—Burke Day

11/12/90

The Story of
CECIL B. DAY
and His Simple
Formula for Success

by
CECIL BURKE DAY, JR.

with
John McCollister

jD | Jonathan David Publishers, Inc.
Middle Village, New York 11379

Jonathan David Publishers, Inc.
68-22 Eliot Avenue
Middle Village, New York 11379

1991 1993 1994 1992 1990
2 4 6 8 10 9 7 5 3 1

Library of Congress Cataloging-in-Publication Data

Day, Cecil Burke.
  Day by Day: the story of Cecil B. Day and his simple formula
for success / by Cecil Burke Day, Jr.; with John McCollister.
     p.   cm.
  Includes bibliographical references and index.
  ISBN 0-8246-0347-8
  1. Success in business—United States. 2. Day, Cecil, 1934-
1978. 3. Businessmen—United States.   I. McCollister, John.   II.
Title.
HF5386.D328   1990
338.7'61647947302'092—dc20
[B]   90-14009
                                                              CIP

Printed in the United States of America

Dedicated to
the three women in my life:
my Grandmother Day,
my mother, Deen,
and my wife,
Sally

CONTENTS

7

IN APPRECIATION

I am indebted to those industrious people at Cecil B. Day Investment Company whose unselfish help contributed tremendously to this book's publication. Among those deserving special praise are: Elisabeth Stone, Charla Canale, Eddie Burnette, Charles Sanders, Carole Smith, Shirley Newell, Barbara Kerr, Woody White, Leslie Furman, Sharon Gordon, Dick Fowler, Helen Falk, Beth Smith, Mary Wallden, Clara Wilkerson and Deen Day Smith.

C.B.D.

In 1972 Cecil took Burke on a six-week trip to the Far East and Australia. They carried only what they wore, had open airline tickets, no lodging reservations and agreed to sleep on park benches if lodging was unavailable. Four weeks into the trip, Cecil and Burke agreed to cut the trip short and return home. Cecil missed his wife, Deen, and Burke longed for his fiancée, Sally (now his wife).

PREFACE

by
Cecil Burke Day, Jr.

The movie title *Back to the Future* holds a new meaning for me. In the movie, a son returns to a time when his parents-to-be have yet to meet; he sees what he already knows is their destiny. For me, writing this book has been every bit of a journey into the past.

Before I could take the first step on that journey, the eagle-eyed and witty Dr. John McCollister taught me an important lesson—when to take off my "son" hat and replace it with my "writer" hat. I did as he instructed and learned many important things.

I looked—for the first time—at Cecil B. Day, as a man, not just as a father. Now, after many months of research, I better understand why other people were so impressed with him.

In my journey into the past, I was forced to recall stories my dad told me about many of the motels constructed along America's interstates. I include here some of these stories, as well as our in-depth discussions about business and life.

In addition to my personal recollections, I learned from the meticulous notes of Gainer Bryan and Dr. John Haggai about things that shaped Cecil Day as a youngster. Crumpled pieces of paper on which Cecil once wrote shed new insights into his uniqueness.

My Uncle Lon shared a library of newspaper clippings, letters and notes about the Day family dating from the mid-1800s until the present. His conscientious efforts not only gave me interesting facts about my dad, but also provided me with the background that helped shaped the personality of the founder of Days Inns.

Help given by the people of Days Inns' marketing and public relations departments was extremely valuable. Telephone discussions and lunches with many who knew Cecil Day were often peppered with stories about my father that I might otherwise have never heard.

Unfortunately, I've not been able to mention in this book every name involved in the story of Days Inns. That cast of characters includes thousands of gutsy, devoted people. I would need volumes to list them all.

This doesn't take anything away from the fact that every person who worked for Cecil Day was important to him. Loyal maids, maintenance people, desk clerks, cooks, waitresses, managers and home office employees—they were all Cecil's heartthrobs. He loved each one more than himself, and made that clear, even to those of us at home. Also, were it not for kind, patient bankers, Days Inns would have never survived the Arab oil embargo of 1973. Cooperative franchisees helped dot the globe with the familiar sunburst Days Inns signs.

After reviewing their many contributions, I can see why my father loved them all so much.

If I've offended anybody by omission, please forgive me. I hope you realize that you are the Days Inns story and that no one person may make that claim alone.

Taking the journey into the past was one thing. Returning from it was another. Reconstructing the events that resulted in this book proves to me beyond any doubt that Cecil Day's formula for success works. The mere fact that this book is in your hands proves my point.

Many times I wanted to pick up my keyboard—computer attached—and toss it out a window in frustration. But I was writing about a man who refused to quit. Whenever I ran into what seemed to be a brick wall, I read the notes available to me and drew from them an unbreakable resolve to finish what I started. That spirit is a Cecil B. Day, Sr., trademark.

I would be remiss in not mentioning those people who served on the book's committee. My mother, Deen Day Smith; brothers Clint, Peyton and Parke; sister Kathie; Uncle Lon; and Cecil Day's close business associates Jo Dollar and Robert L. Williams.

Finally, I thank my dear wife, Sally, who patiently read and reread this manuscript without complaining, and my sons, Brandon, Jonathan and Daniel for not bouncing the basketball or yelling outside my office while I wrote this book.

FOREWORD

by
Michael A. Leven
Former President and Chief Operating Officer
Days Inns of America, Inc.

I never knew Cecil Day . . . yet I know Cecil Day. I discovered this when I proudly served as Days Inns president until May, 1990. How I ever came to that honorable position always intrigued me.

In April of 1985, by a stroke of good luck, I began serving as president of Days Inns. Little did I know then that my luck strongly resembled the kind of process that built Cecil's company and his reputation.

Three months earlier, I was standing at a pay phone in New York returning telephone calls while waiting for a plane. At the bottom of the stack was a message from an old friend I hadn't seen or spoken with since 1978, when he was released from a significant position in my former company. Although I had about 15 messages and all seemed very important, I moved his to the top because I thought he needed help. Why would he have called on this particular day after all these years?

He answered the phone, we exchanged pleasantries, and then he asked, "Would you have any interest in the president's job at Days Inns? My boss is on the board and, if so, he will meet with you today."

Well, the rest is history but for one thing: Why did I pull out that particular message from all the others?

Somehow I believe there *was* another influence, another "invisible hand." Could it have been Cecil's? His faith's? His legacy's? I never knew until I finished reading *Day by Day*. Now I know!

Shortly after I came to the Day Building, a long-standing employee came to my office to let me know that Cecil's picture was in a closet. Then this employee asked something of me: Would I hang it somewhere so everyone could see it?

"Of course," I replied. We hung Cecil's portrait in a most visible place—in our headquarter's lobby, next to the elevators. Why? I believed everyone in the Day Building had a job because of Cecil's vision. I wasn't aware how similar the values were between founder (Cecil) and manager (me) until more time passed.

A cadre of competent employees, still there, had survived seven years of different directions without Cecil's leadership. They yearned for a return to the basic tenets which created a successful company. A dissident group of franchisees waited like hungry wolves to assert or renew their rights and opportunities which had been restricted or removed since Cecil's death in 1978.

As I listened, it occurred to me that all of them only wanted the company and themselves to be successful in partnership.

Resolving the conflict was easy. The foundation that Cecil and his family had built was so strong that even when the house burned the foundation remained intact.

We rebuilt it with the same spirit, the same gusto, the same values, the same ethics and the same sense of fairness on which the company was founded. We opened opportunities to all and let our employees walk through the front door again.

Change is never easy. But returning to a methodology that *everyone* wanted was not very difficult.

I am not an entrepreneur like Cecil Day. Perhaps I was fortunate to be one of the executors of his mission. That mission remains not only to make Days as the "McDonald's of the hospitality industry," but also—and of more importance—is to keep Days as an exemplary company which sets the highest concerns for its employees, its franchisees, its guests and its community.

It is to see Days as an organization which millions of people will honor with their confidence and their patronage, an institution that proves our economic system is the fairest and the best.

I wish I could take credit for where Days Inns is today, but that credit must go to Cecil, his family, his beliefs and his courage.

I can only be thankful that I once worked in his shadow.

Carol Thompson, a worker in the Days corporate homeless program, is shown with John D. Snodgrass, current president of Days Inns of America, Inc.

INTRODUCTION

by
John D. Snodgrass
President and Chief Operating Officer
Days Inns of America, Inc.

When I was offered the opportunity to become president of Days Inns on May 3, 1990, I had occasion to reflect on my experiences of the past ten years with this company. Having served under three different owners and two presidents, I have witnessed many changes.

Change is inevitable. But one thing that has not changed, one thing that transcends all of the CEOs, COOs, the buyouts and stock options, is the basic philosophy set down by this company's founder, Cecil B. Day.

I never had the privilege of knowing Mr. Day. But I have heard story after story and in each one has been the fact that Cecil Day followed a strict set of values and ethics. His value system was never altered by circumstances. I believe that his principles have served as inspiration for all who have held the executive office of this corporation. And all who have been touched by his legacy are better for it.

What are those principles? Cecil Day believed in treating Days Inn guests fairly. He knew they wanted a genuine value. It was his view that customers warranted a safe, comfortable and clean room—at prices lower than a guest would be expected to pay elsewhere. He not only dreamed it was possible—he proved it. He not only believed it should happen—he made it happen.

His vision resulted in a company with a personality. A company unafraid to take risks in the name of community service. A company which relates with sensitivity to its employees, its franchisees and every community it touches.

Since assuming the leadership role at Days, I have developed a deeper appreciation for foundations. The foundation laid down by Cecil Day. The foundation my friend Michael Leven inherited and successfully built upon. The foundation now entrusted to me—one I am proud to embrace and vow to cherish.

In the years since Mr. Day's death, this company has created and instituted revolutionary hiring practices. As a result, senior citizens, the physically impaired and the homeless have opportunities to profit from their contributions to the work force. The company contributes to the quality of life for others by supporting the arts and organizations such as the Juvenile Diabetes Foundation. Individual Days properties contribute as well. Our corporate office mailroom is filled-to-overflowing with letters describing individual acts of kindness performed by property managers and employees. Benevolence is contagious—our customers thank us by staying at Days again.

A sense of fair play is strong within Days ranks. The needs of franchisees are very important, as well as the issues which affect them. For example, the growing population of Asian-American hoteliers is still met with prejudice in the business world as a whole—but not at Days. The first Asian-American Hotel/Motel Owners Association was formed with the support of Days to seek solutions to the unique problems facing this community.

Many business leaders today subscribe to the philosophy

that "good guys finish last." We disagree. Our results don't indicate that philosophy as true. Cecil Day built a solid, successful family-owned business based on Judeo-Christian ethics. When the Day family sold the company and franchising escalated again, the company experienced explosive growth, while keeping the basic philosophies of its founder in mind.

We will stay on that track, continuing to grow nationally and internationally. We will continue to diversify the Days lodging brand to meet the needs of the traveling public. And we will remain sensitive to the needs of our franchise owners and the world around us.

I heard a long-standing Days franchisee remark, "This is a company with a heart." That sentiment seems to be one few corporations our size can identify with these days— more importantly, support and carry out.

What Cecil Day dreamed of and accomplished, we, the heirs of his legacy, will proudly carry forward. His dreams as shown in *Day by Day* are ours to fulfill today . . . and in the years yet-to-come.

TRIBUTES
TO
CECIL B. DAY

Paul Harvey:

As much as Cecil Day was so much fun as a friend, this loving narrative, read one chapter every bedtime, will keep you feeling good day by day.

Coretta Scott King:

Cecil B. Day was not only one of the nation's most dynamic and creative entrepreneurs, he was a great-hearted business leader, whose exceptional humanitarian concern set the highest standards of corporate social responsibility. His many contributions to building a better America stand as a shining example of conscience and compassion.

Ronald Reagan:

When our nation's forefathers drafted the Constitution, they had people like Cecil Day in mind. Building on its foundation, Cecil demonstrated how the American dream can be fulfilled without compromising a sense of values. His business motto—"A deal is not a deal unless it's a good deal for *both* parties"—was, and still is, an essential attitude daring entrepreneurs should embrace.

Kemmons Wilson:
Founder, Holiday Inns

Cecil Day proved that dreams, when combined with positive action, are reachable. What set him apart from other dreamers is that he put into action his religious, heartfelt convictions and actually *made* these principles work *for* him. His honorable business conduct, his charitable grace and devoted love for God and man made Days Inns a successful reality. Reading Cecil's simple formula for success as shown in this book is time and money well spent.

Jimmy Carter:

Cecil Day's rags-to-riches story epitomizes the American dream-come-true. He demonstrated by example how a rich family life and professional success can be achieved based on biblical principles.

Curtis Cheshire:
Former Group Vice President,
Trust Company Bank

If more people conducted their business as did Cecil Day, we would have a sounder, more efficient, trustworthy environment in which to conduct business, which would lead to a better economy for everyone.

Gerald R. Ford:

Cecil Day, Sr., was a stalwart believer in and fighter for

the highest American principles. *Day by Day* emphatically tells his story of success in the business marketplace.

Truett Cathy:
Founder and Chairman, Chic-fil-A

Cecil Day . . . a great guy with a tremendous amount of faith and dedication to our Lord. He is one person I can truly say *knew* God, rather than just knew *of* God.

Richard M. Nixon:

Cecil Day learned as a Marine Corps platoon leader that things don't just happen—you've got to make them happen. That attitude, combined with a solid sense of values, made him what he had to be in creating what is now the world's third largest motel chain—Days Inns. Cecil's simple formula for success is revealed by his son in the inspiring pages of *Day by Day.*

Billy Graham:

Cecil Day's life demonstrated that biblical principles are necessities in the business marketplace and offer simple guidelines for a happy life. He proved the Bible a most effective textbook for business administration and triumphantly lived what he learned from it.

Joe Rogers, Jr.:
President, Waffle House

As a man of vision, compassion and talent, Cecil Day could always figure out a way to do something when everyone else was stumped. . . . A man's strength shines through in difficult times and Cecil's certainly did. We continued doing

business with him on a handshake and he always lived up
to it.

Harold Northrop:
President and CEO,
Callaway Gardens

Cecil Day was a kind and gentle warrior. His values were
shaped by "The Book," his life inspired and enriched by
"the land."

Andrew Young:
Mayor of Atlanta

I highly recommend this personal, intimate account of
a true Christian gentleman. To me, Cecil Day represented
the true spirit of human generosity and compassion. He was
an extremely successful businessman who never compro-
mised his religious values for career gain. Cecil Day and
his family have meant a great deal to me and the city of
Atlanta through the years.

George Busbee:
Former Governor of Georgia

Cecil Day's life demonstrated the "American Dream" at
its very best. He was a highly successful businessman whose
journey to the top in the business world was distinguished
by hard work, and total dedication to his family, his state
and nation, and to his God.

Dr. John Haggai:
Founder and President,
Haggai Institute for Advanced Leadership Training

Cecil Day made decisions on the basis of "Is it right?

Is it consistent with my Christian commitment?" When the oil embargo threatened the survival of his real estate empire, his calm verified his faith and commitment. And at the same time, he impacted for good and for God scores of nations. More than 8,000 leaders on five continents applaud this man's influence on their lives.

Sam Nunn:
U.S. Senator

Cecil Day was a businessman of great vision and ability, but he was more than that. Even at times when the very survival of his enterprises was in great danger, he held firmly to his Christian principles, and *tithed* both in the difficult days of starting up his business and during the depths of recessions that threatened to bankrupt him. He left a thriving institution that serves a real need, but he also left an example of morality and generosity that demonstrates how vision can be turned into practical economical success that benefits customers, employees and communities.

Carl E. Sanders:
Former Governor of Georgia

Cecil B. Day was one of the finest men I ever knew. Success to him was helping others, not personal gain. By virtue of his values in life, he will never be forgotten.

Ivan Allen, Jr.:
CEO, Ivan Allen Company

During the Arab oil embargo, the travel industry suffered significantly, and Days Inns was no exception. During this time, largely due to the outstanding reputation of Cecil B. Day, the Ivan Allen Company was willing to extend additional credit terms to help ride through this period. Our confidence was certainly justified. When things returned to normal, Days Inns continued to be an outstanding customer in every respect.

Bill Bright:
Founder and President,
Campus Crusade for Christ

Cecil Day was a rare combination of a genius in the business realm and a faithful ambassador to our Lord. His remarkable ability was demonstrated by the phenomenal success of the business which bears his name, a creative idea he executed so brilliantly.

Scott Hudgens:
Chairman, Scott Hudgens Companies

When Cecil worked for me, I never had to go to him for an explanation about anything. If one was needed, he would be there before anyone knew about it. He had the ability to look into the future and see things which were coming to pass in the real estate field—like Days Inns.

Dr. James P. Wesberry:
Executive Director,
The Lord's Day Alliance of the United States

I had the privilege of knowing not just Cecil Day, but his father with whom I attended Mercer University. His father's example made Cecil an example for aspiring people in all fields. Cecil was a brilliant, gifted, kind and Christian gentleman of the highest rank and order. And now one of his sons, Burke, shares some of Cecil's secrets for success in this fine book, *Day by Day*. It's a thrilling one!

Norman Vincent Peale:

Mr. Day was a highly successful Christian man who applied positive principles in developing what is now the world's third largest motel chain. I'll never forget his attitude of "keep on keeping on." This book by his son Burke, *Day by Day*, will tell each reader how to be successful in the truest sense.

Pat Robertson:
CEO, The Christian Broadcasting Network
"The 700 Club"

What stands out most in my mind about Cecil Day is his great humility. Just before he appeared on the "700 Club," Cecil asked me an unusual question: "Where's the bathroom?" Later, I was told he was seen there kneeling in prayer. Even as the successful and enormously talented man he was, Cecil sought out God first—even in the most unorthodox places. That's humility.

1

Dare to Dare

Cecil Day's entire life, personal and professional, was an example worth following, because he was following an Example worth following.

I'll never forget his kite flying experience at the age of seven, and I'll bet you won't.

—Paul Harvey

Seven-year-old Cecil Day, a yet-to-be CEO, enjoyed "being in the saddle."

He was truly a great man who left me something far more than money—a good, clean name and an appreciation of the true values in life, based on Christian principles.

—Cecil B. Day,
remembering his father

Cecil Day's young eyes opened wide as he watched his new red kite zigzag across the deep blue sky of his hometown—Savannah, Georgia. He laughed out loud each time it dove toward the ground, then suddenly jetted back up. The long white knotted tail slithered like a snake once it regained its altitude.

But that wasn't enough. The seven-year-old wanted it to soar higher and farther, so he added two more balls of string to the end of the one he held in his small hand. The kite sailed higher . . . higher . . . until it became smaller than a speck against the clouds.

"Time for dinner, son," yelled his father. Rev. Lon Day, a Baptist minister, shouted from inside the white clapboard house. "Hurry up. Supper's gonna get cold."

But Cecil didn't answer.

Rev. Day stepped outside. He saw his young son sitting in the front yard, still clutching a string in his hand. He was sobbing.

"What's wrong, son?" asked Rev. Day as he knelt beside the boy.

"My kite, Daddy. It's lost," lamented Cecil, as tears ran down his cheeks.

Rev. Day's eyes followed the string that rose slightly upward into the sky. "How do you know it's lost?" he asked, putting his hand on Cecil's shoulder.

"Look. . . . " His little hand shook as he pointed to the sky. "You can't see it anymore."

"Hummmmmmmmmmm. Tell me, can you feel a tug on the string?" his father asked with a smile in his voice.

"Yes, sir," said Cecil, "but it's gone. I still can't see it."

"Son, hold tight to the cord. As long as you feel it pulling, you know it's there," Rev. Day concluded, "just like God works when He tugs at your heart."

Young Cecil leaped to his feet, wiped away a tear, then began reeling in the string. Gradually the soaring kite came back into view. In less than ten minutes the kite was safely in his hand.

He probably didn't realize it at the time, but Rev. Day had made a powerful impression upon his son—one that would guide him throughout his life, both professionally and personally.

Keep on Keepin' on

Cecil's father was an excellent teacher in terms of establishing a proper sense of values. Years later, during his early teens, Cecil had a paper delivery route in Macon. On one particularly hot, muggy August afternoon, when vapor rose off the asphalt road, Cecil pedaled his bike up a steep hill. Halfway up the hill, waiting for his son, as he frequently did, was Rev. Day, holding a bottle of cold soda in his hands.

Cecil downed the soda quickly. His father walked beside him as the young boy pedaled the paper-laden bike.

"Keep on keepin' on!" Rev. Day shouted. "Keep on keepin' on."

"That small refreshment and encouragement helped me get over that hump of my delivery route," Cecil recalled later. "Dad was always a great cheerleader."

Rev. Day had a habit of encouraging both Cecil and his older brother, Lon, when they tried various business ventures. Once when the two young men sold Cokes from a wagon to construction workers, Rev. Day supported their efforts.

He taught them that going into business—any business—was a stewardship. He likened the businessman to a trustee in charge of a trust. "You are the caretaker," he told them, "and you must do whatever you can to make it a success, else it will fail."

Sometimes that meant sacrificing things close to your heart. That had been made exceptionally clear to Cecil a few years earlier. Cecil had received a pet goose as a present. Every day after school, he rushed home to feed and take care of the ever-honking gosling. To Cecil, the goose's "HONK" was merely its way of talking. To the neighbors, however, it was a hair-raising nuisance that kept them awake at night.

Beside the complaints raised by the neighbors, the Days had other problems. Rev. Day's health was failing. He could no longer continue pastoring a church full-time and had to retire. Medical expenses bit hard into the family's budget. Rev. Day's meager pension of $41 a month was hardly enough to buy food. There was only one solution. His mother and father killed the goose while Cecil was at school and cooked it for the family meal.

When Cecil returned home and discovered what had happened, he dashed out of the house. "You murdered my pet," he screamed as he ran down the street.

His father chased after him, caught up with him, and sat him down. They spoke heart-to-heart about the dilemma. Rev. Day begged for forgiveness.

Young Cecil nodded his head. "But, please . . . don't make me eat any," said Cecil, trying to fight back the tears. "I loved him so much."

The Lesson of Tithing

Eight-year-old Cecil sat uncharacteristically still in the front row of Immanuel Church in Savannah. His father was not standing in the pulpit that night. It was a revival service in his church that occurred about once each year for a week and was led by a visiting minister.

Cecil looked at the towering guest speaker, James Wesberry from Atlanta. The preacher spoke forcefully about stewardship and how God expects much from those to whom He has given. Cecil leaned forward and listened to each word.

Offering plates were handed to the church's deacons who readied them for passing around the pews.

Cecil wiggled in his seat, then dug deep into his pockets. He pulled out his only two coins—a quarter and a nickel.

As the collection plate neared him, he looked at the large quarter in his left hand; then he looked at the small nickel in the other. He kept looking in one palm, then the next.

When the offering plate reached him, he wrestled once more about which coin should go in the plate—the shiny quarter or the nickel? Finally, he placed the quarter in the plate, passed it to the person next to him and smiled with relief.

As the sermon ended, Wesberry challenged those who had never accepted Christ as their Savior to step forward. Cecil's stomach felt unusually different. Something inside of him urged him to walk forward and make public his declaration of faith.

Cecil wondered if taking such a step might hurt his father's feelings. Since his dad was the church's full-time pastor, would it embarrass him?

Yet the gnawing inside grew more fierce.

Piano music filled the church during the invitational, and Wesberry stepped down to floor level. With outstretched hands he greeted those walking to the front of the sanctuary.

Cecil felt like a balloon close to popping. He leaped off the seat and ran forward.

Warmly greeted by Wesberry, Cecil took a tiny step that forever directed his longer strides. His father was teary-eyed later that very night as he baptized Cecil.

"I'm very proud of you, son," he said as he immersed his son.

A few nights later, Cecil joined his father, who drove Wesberry to the Savannah train station. The train whistle pierced the air summoning all passengers to board. Cecil watched his father and Wesberry shake hands.

Wesberry started up the steps into the train, then stopped. He turned and gestured for Cecil to approach him.

Cecil walked to the edge of the steps and looked up at the Atlanta-bound preacher.

"Young man," boomed Wesberry, "I want you to take this and split it evenly with your brother."

Cecil stretched up and took what the preacher offered. His eyes popped open and his jaw dropped.

"Dad! Look! A five-dollar bill! I get to keep half of it, too." Then he paused for a second and said, "God has given me *ten times* what I gave Him!"

Death of "a Great Man"

Rev. Day's health grew worse over the years. His activities were limited to playing Monopoly with Cecil from his bedside. Not only did these games allow Cecil to know his father even better, they also taught him the basics of real estate. He quickly caught on to the process of acquiring property first, building income-producing structures on it, then collecting rent from those who landed on his color-coded properties dotting the game board.

On December 20, 1949, 15-year-old Cecil Day wore a borrowed black suit to his father's funeral. The coat sleeves hung limp over his hands, and the pant cuffs raised to Cecil's calves whenever he sat down.

His mother, Kathleen, arranged to borrow not just the suit, but the $2,000 it cost to bury Rev. Day.

Many times following his father's death, Cecil still felt the urge to share something with his dad. Sometimes, if he had some important news to tell, he ran to his father's favorite chair—the one in which he sat to think and write sermons. But now the chair was empty.

Cecil remembered his father as "a great man who left me something far more than money—a good, clean name and an appreciation of the true values in life based on Christian principles. He was a servant of both God and man— the highest station a person can attain."

A Remarkable Woman

Kathleen Day faced heavy odds. Although educated as a teacher, she possessed a keen sense for business. Now she had to put that gift to use to earn a living for the family in a male-dominated business world. An equal rights amendment was only a dream, but Kathleen didn't need one. Instead, she defied the thinking of the '40s and plowed into the mainstream of business.

She sold ads for *The Christian Index*—a statewide newspaper. Often, she outsold her male coworkers and brought home as much as $100 a week. But there were many weeks when she did not. At home, the subject of money was the main topic of conversation. Prior to her husband's death, she had converted the dining room and sun parlor of the house in Savannah into extra bedrooms. The garage became an apartment. She rented out each room to tourists. On more than one occasion Cecil asked: "Where will I sleep tonight?"

Taking a lesson from her late husband, Mrs. Day sold their home in Savannah and used the money to purchase a two-bedroom house in Macon that was currently rented to tenants. She and Cecil lived in an apartment in Macon, while the house she bought brought in more income than did selling newspaper ads. But although she was successful in renting the house, the rental income was not enough to provide a livable wage.

On a small table cluttered with papers, Kathleen Day meticulously entered numbers into a ledger book. Her face grew red, and she threw down her pencil in frustration. "Cecil, we just don't have enough money," she moaned. "There's not enough for us even to eat." She buried her face in her palms and wept.

Without saying a word, 16-year-old Cecil reached inside his school knapsack and handed his mother some crude drawings.

"What's this?" she asked, regaining her composure.

"I have an idea that should work," said Cecil. "I think we can subdivide this house into a duplex. We can rent out one half to pay the mortgage. That means we live free in the other half."

Kathleen wiped the tears from her eyes and studied Cecil's set of plans. For the first time in months her eyes showed a glimmer of hope.

"I think we can do this for about one thousand dollars," said Cecil.

By ten o'clock the next morning, Kathleen and Cecil were in a banker's office requesting a loan to finance the small project.

The banker looked at the rough drawings without showing any expression of acceptance or rejection.

"Hrumph," he grunted. "Excuse me. I've got to get another opinion." He left the office still holding the plans in his hand.

When he returned, he handed the plans back to Mrs. Day. "These drawings are quite good," he said. "They show real potential. But I won't lend you one thousand for them...."

"Well," interrupted a solemn Kathleen, "thank you very much for your time." She stood up to leave. But the banker wasn't through talking.

". . . These plans are so good, we're willing to loan you *this* amount." He handed her an envelope.

Kathleen sat down. She opened the envelope and smiled. "Twelve hundred, fifty dollars!" she said. "Thank you, sir."

"Don't mention it. If you need more, let me know," said the banker.

That afternoon Cecil and his mother hired carpenters to start construction. Young Cecil supervised them and explained his plans as they went along. By the end of the month Cecil and his mother proudly admired their new duplex. A tenant's car was already parked on the right-hand side.

Cecil and his mother continued to live rent-free over the next few years. To help with the family expenses, Cecil worked 40 hours each week at a variety of jobs while attending high school.

Cecil actually liked working. He didn't like school, however. He was caught cutting classes at least 70 times during his junior and senior years. He opted, instead, to visit friends or the local pool hall.

By the grace of God and the faculty, Cecil finally graduated from high school at the June 1952 commencement. When he stretched out his hand to receive his diploma, Kathleen bowed her head and muttered a silent prayer of thanks.

Cecil Day Meets Deen

Although he was far from being class valedictorian, Cecil was smart enough to realize that a college education was necessary for success in business. He was permitted to enroll at Mercer University—a Baptist college in Macon—partly because his father had attended there years earlier.

At first it looked as though Cecil would be caught up in the college spirit. He pledged the SAE fraternity and became involved with campus activities. But his old habit of cutting classes returned.

Instead of attending a lecture in English 101, Day was sitting with a friend in the school's gymnasium watching co-eds play basketball. One particular brunette caught his attention.

"Do you see that girl over there?" he asked.

"Yeah," his friend replied. "But if you have any idea about dating her, forget it. She's already pinned to a guy who just graduated."

"She's one of the most beautiful girls I've ever seen," said Cecil, ignoring his friend's advice. "I'd like to meet her."

"Forget it," said his friend. "I told you she's almost married. Besides, she a year older than you."

Cecil never took his eyes off her. "What's her name?" he asked.

"Uldine . . . Uldine Smith," sighed his friend. "But, Cecil, you don't have a chance."

"Wanna bet?" asked Cecil.

Four months later, Uldine showed her sorority sisters Cecil's SAE pin on her dress.

Cecil's romantic life may have been bliss, but his grades were dismal. Eventually his grades dipped so low that he was booted out of Mercer.

Cecil's ambition was to attend Georgia Tech. Now his odds of doing that were lower than ever.

When Cecil received word of his abrupt dismissal, Uldine was on an extended sorority trip with friends to the western United States, Canada and Mexico. The trip was somewhat of an obligation, since she had recently been elected as president of her Alpha Delta Pi sorority for the following year.

Cecil was never one to lie down and quit. He eventually found one way he could become admitted to Georgia Tech in spite of his not-too-spectacular track record at Mercer. Georgia Tech, he learned, allowed veterans an opportunity to attend on a one-quarter trial basis.

The ringing telephone in Uldine's hotel room interrupted a conversation with her friends about the joys of meeting June Allyson, Jimmy Stewart and Edward G. Robinson all in the same day. Even the older girls in the room could hear the angry voice of her father on the other end of the line.

"Deen, that Cecil Day has been here, and that young man has marriage on his mind," blared Mr. Smith. "Young lady, you're not getting married until you get out of school!"

"Awwwww, you know I wouldn't do that, Daddy," answered Uldine with the sort of sugary tone specifically designed to soothe the hearts of all men—even fathers.

"Good," said her much more relaxed father.

When Uldine hung up the phone, she smiled at her sorority sisters who were packing the luggage for their trip to Mexico the next morning. "Marriage? Did he say 'marriage'?"

The last piece of luggage was placed on top of the automobile with "Canada, California and Mexico or Bust" painted on its windows just as another call came for Uldine.

"Guess who just joined the Marines?" shouted Cecil.

Uldine's mouth dropped open and her thin, dark brows furrowed. "When do you leave?" she asked.

"July twenty-first," said Cecil.

"Cecil, that's less than a month from now. And . . . I . . . this trip won't be completed until August," Deen pleaded. "And when I get back, I have responsibilities. . . . "

"I want you to come home and marry me *now*," interrupted Cecil.

"But Cecil . . . what about my education . . . ?"

"I promise you that you'll finish someday," Cecil said.

"And Dad? What about my dad?"

"I'll promise him that somehow you'll finish college," Cecil said with a stern voice that Deen had not heard before.

"My friends . . . my sorority . . . what will I say to them?"

"Deen," blurted Cecil into the mouthpiece, "you can't have it both ways." He slammed down the phone.

"I blew it!" Cecil said to himself. "I'm going to enter the Marine Corps a single man." He accepted the fact that Deen could wipe his name off her list of suitors while he was in the service protecting her right to do so.

For one of the rare times in his life, Cecil's "gut reaction" was wrong. On July 12, Cecil met Uldine who had driven back to Columbus, Georgia. Cecil and Uldine were married four days later. His mother served as an official witness to the informal ceremony in a tiny Baptist Church in Columbus.

"I'll never forget," confessed Cecil 24 years later. "Deen looked at me with those big brown eyes, scared to death. I gazed down at her like I knew exactly what I was doing and gave her that 'Don't worry about a thing' look. I don't think she ever knew how scared *I* was."

Following a four-day honeymoon, Cecil kissed his young bride good-bye and walked up the steps of a Greyhound bus bound for Parris Island, South Carolina.

The Marine Recruit

When the bus, loaded with new recruits, arrived at the camp at six o'clock in the morning, a muscular, heavy-jawed drill instructor literally marched up the steps. He paced up and down the aisle a few times without saying a word, burning each recruit with a stare, and slapping his right hand against his thigh with every other step.

When he reached the front of the bus, he abruptly turned, stood erect, and with piercing eyes looked at each recruit again.

"All right, knuckleheads," he shouted. "You'd better say 'good-bye' to God and everybody else, because when you cross that bridge and get on that island, your butts belong to me!"

"In that brief moment," Day said later, "I believed every word he said."

While on the bus, every recruit looked different. Some had beards; a few wore mustaches; others had shaggy hair. That all changed before noon. Every recruit now wore the same uniform and sported the same haircut—that is if you could call a shaved head a "haircut."

Cecil scored highest on his GCT (General Classification Test). He was made a platoon leader. Although he did not have the authority of a drill instructor, he bore the responsibility of his platoon's operations.

During the first week of basic training, one recruit in his platoon was caught by the drill instructor with some "pogey bait"—Marine jargon for a forbidden luxury (usually candy).

The drill instructor ordered Day to call his platoon outside and to stand at attention. Day and his group stood there for a solid hour in the near 100-degree heat. Their shirts darkened from perspiration, and gnats filled the air. Several flew up Day's nose, but he ignored them. To slap or kill one of the sand gnats, which bite as though they have teeth, meant, according to the drill sergeant, digging a 10'x10'x10' hole and burying the deceased.

Day felt relieved when he saw the drill instructor out of the corner of his eye. The D.I. cast darting glances at the platoon, then stood right in front of Day's face. The lip of his hat brushed up against Day's forehead.

"JACOBS!" bellowed the D.I., while still looking at Cecil.

"Yes, SIR!" snapped the Marine.

"What was that you had in your bunk, Jacobs?"

"Pogey bait, SIR!" shouted Jacobs.

"And were you supposed to have that in your bunk, Jacobs?"

"No, SIR," yelled Jacobs.

The D.I. walked a few steps away from Cecil, singled out Jacobs and stared him dead in the eye. Silently, he slowly walked back toward Cecil. Without warning, the D.I. raised his fist and smacked him in the side, severely bruising a rib.

Cecil nearly folded over, then quickly resumed his erect position. He continued to stare straight ahead. He said nothing.

The D.I. returned to the front of Cecil, leaned close and shouted, "Day! Watch your ship, boy. And everyone on it. If they screw up one more time, I'll chew your butt from here to Georgia and back!" The sergeant started to walk away, then turned for one last reminder. "It's your butt, Day. Do you hear me?"

"Yes, SIR!" bellowed Day.

Return to College

Immediately after basic training, Cecil sent for his wife to join him. But their first home was anything but the ivy-covered cottage pictured in fairy tales. It was a 9'x14' trailer—sans bathroom. It was crowded quarters for two; even more so when their first child—Cecil Burke Day, Jr.— was born in April 1954.

Cecil completed his active duty in two years. The Corps had given him things he would always treasure. One was discipline. But equally important at that moment was the ticket to Georgia Tech and a chance to attend the college of his dreams.

Day carried 15 hours each quarter over the next three

years. His family had increased by one—Kathleen Smith Day. He worked 60 hours a week and budgeted his time between family, church and study.

Cecil Day graduated from Georgia Tech in 1958 with only the minimum passing grades. But he made it. Many of his fellow classmates signed on with major corporations; Day, however, set his sights on his favorite enterprise—real estate.

He studied hard and passed his real estate broker's exam on his first try in 1959. He and Deen proudly put a "Broker" sign in the front yard of his small house in Atlanta.

For a solid year he worked as "Cecil B. Day, Broker." But something happened that he never expected. Something for which neither school nor experience had prepared him.

He flopped.

This time, the kite was gone.

2

Find a Need
and Fill It

Cecil Day learned as a Marine Corps platoon leader
that things don't just happen. You've got to make them
happen. That attitude, combined with a solid sense of
values, made him the leader he had to be.

—Richard M. Nixon

During an interview, a reporter asked, "Mr. Day, what advice do you have for those who want to make a lot of money?" Cecil replied: "Find a need, then fill it."

A deal is not a deal unless it's a good deal for both parties.
                                                    —Cecil B. Day

He was 24 years old, a husband, father of two with another on the way, and a failure in business—hardly an enviable professional station in life.

More dust than money lined Cecil Day's pockets in 1959. Sure, he had plenty of vision, but most of his friends and associates considered Cecil just another dreamer with little promise. Nonetheless, Cecil never lost faith in himself. Neither did a major Atlanta real estate developer.

For about one year, Cecil worked for Ernie Kepler—owner of Dolphin Homes of Atlanta, a housing construction firm. Cecil, of course, worked for a modest salary. However, income from a salary never stimulated Cecil Day. He, instead, preferred to work solely on a commission. A salary, according to Cecil, only set a limit on the amount of money he could make.

Cecil once suggested to Ernie Kepler that he work not for a salary, but for a "draw against sales commissions." This, thought Day, would be a perfect compromise. Day needed a steady income to pay his bills; working for commissions would increase his earning potential. In addition, this would inspire him to work even harder for Kepler.

Kepler thought seriously about it but chose to refuse Day's offer. Perhaps Ernie Kepler, out of concern, was afraid that Cecil would once again get himself buried under increasing financial obligations. Some might say that Kepler wanted to keep more of the profits for his company. Whatever the reason, Cecil respected Ernie's decision and remained friends with him until his dying day. "After all," Cecil often said, "a deal is not a deal unless it's a good deal for both parties."

Career Objectives

Before failing in business that year as Cecil B. Day, Broker, Cecil had juggled a few other enterprises as well. He earned money to put food on the table by drafting house plans and engineering air-conditioning systems for offices, homes, even a jail. He also started a heating and air-conditioning business with two of Deen's uncles. Together they chose as the name for their company "DASS"—an acronym for Day, Smith and Smith.

Twice each week Cecil drove between Atlanta and Macon in order to sell and design air-conditioning systems which his in-laws installed. One appointment in particular was a turning point in his life.

Cecil had just sold a unit to a successful builder in Atlanta. He had earlier told the builder about his less-than-spectacular venture into real estate. The builder seemed to appreciate Cecil's honesty. "There are too many people in this world who are afraid to admit they failed in something," he said. "I admire you for owning up to it."

As the builder was signing his name to the contract, he casually mentioned to Cecil, "You ought to talk with a guy named Scott Hudgens. He's opening another real estate office and is looking for a broker."

Cecil's initial reaction was to decline the suggestion. Those golden dreams offered by real estate had not come true for him in the past. Why should he try it again? But rather than throw up his hands and surrender to his humiliating experience, Cecil agreed to speak with Hudgens. That night he called Scott Hudgens; they set up a meeting for the next afternoon.

The meeting was short and to the point. Cecil was willing to work for Hudgens, but only on that same "draw-against-sales commissions" basis he had offered earlier to Ernie Kepler. In any business other than real estate, this would be called an advance against salary.

Scott Hudgens listened. He liked Cecil's self-confidence. "I'll accept this," said Hudgens, slapping his hand on the table and smiling.

"At no time will you be exposed to more than one year in arrears," pledged Cecil. The two shook hands in agreement. The next day, Cecil took down from the front of his house the sign that read: "Cecil B. Day, Broker."

Scott Hudgens' Influence

Day's first six months with Scott Hudgens passed quickly. Cecil sold much more than either he or Hudgens expected. When another young salesman, Felix Cochran, was brought into the Hudgens sales force, Cecil now had a friendly competitor. By trying to outsell the other, each propelled himself even more.

Their first year together was spectacular both for the company and for the two energetic young salesmen. Felix sold one million dollars of real estate; Cecil sold one and a half million. The next year, Cecil sold two million; Felix bettered him by $100,000.

Day quickly learned that competition was healthy, provided you didn't intend to smother your competitor. Competition gave Day the added zip to selling.

Business competition to Day was akin to a friendly game of checkers, and he opted for as many "kings" as he could earn.

Cecil also discovered that successful selling was contagious. The formula was simple. A sale generated self-confidence; self-confidence generated daring; daring generated fresh ideas; fresh ideas generated more sales. Buyers were much more interested in spending money on a product presented by a salesperson who was self-confident.

Day learned a lot from Scott Hudgens. He studied his investment plan of buying property far removed from established areas and waiting for Atlanta to grow toward the edge of his property. Suddenly, its value shot skyward. Hudgens sold it for several times his investment.

Two years after joining Scott Hudgens, Day was running the sales office and, with Hudgens' permission, formed for himself the Southside Development Corporation through which he bought and developed vacant land.

His enthusiasm for buying surpassed his capital, however. In only a few months he had committed himself to a $30,000 short-term note. It was a financial drain that sucked all available funds from his new company. He sold off some of the non-income-producing land; on a remaining piece of property he built a quadraplex.

The income from this single-roofed, four-unit building produced what Day needed most—cash. Soon he had enough to put a down payment on an entire subdivision of duplexes— 72 of them. Added to the four-unit complex he already had, Cecil Day now owned 148 rental units.

But like the day when he was a kid flying a kite with only one ball of string, this wasn't enough. Instead of more string, Cecil wanted more cash so he could build more. He wanted to build his own apartment complex. For this he needed even more cash.

For a year and a half Day struggled to find a bank to

finance his project. Finally, one bank agreed to give him a construction loan.

Now that he had the cash, he had only one other problem. Cecil Day knew nothing about building an apartment complex.

Quickly, Cecil asked a builder-friend, Tom Fuqua, for help. Fuqua accepted the challenge. It was the start of a long relationship in which Tom Fuqua built nearly everything Cecil financed.

By 1962, Cecil was offered the job as vice president of Scott Hudgens' company. It was a tempting offer. The title and large salary would offer security. But security was never foremost among Cecil's values. After much prayer, Cecil told his friend Scott that this was not for him. Instead, he revealed to Scott Hudgens the plans for developing his own properties.

Less than six months later, in February 1963, Cecil and Scott shook hands. They parted as friends, as Cecil headed again into the world of self-empoyment in real estate. This time, however, he was better equipped than he was back in '59. Not only did he have some necessary training experience, he also took Tom Fuqua and two others with him. There was something else Cecil had at this time. He now owned over a million dollars worth of land and income property.

Cecil was no longer interested in taking a chance on pure speculation. He agreed with Mark Twain who wrote: "There are two times in a man's life when he should not speculate—when he can't afford it, and when he can." Instead, Cecil pledged to himself that he would never go into a business venture unless the odds were in his favor.

To manage, run and operate his apartments, Cecil wanted someone who was experienced, frugal, trustworthy and efficient. He knew of the perfect person. He hired his mother.

For the next six years, Cecil Day continued building

income-producing properties. During this time he introduced a new, two-word concept to the rental market that sent him soaring to even greater heights of success. That heretofore unknown term was: "budget-luxury." It was clearly the right idea for the right time.

In 1963, two distinct rental choices dominated Atlanta— one was high rent; the other was low rent. The forgotten person in all this was the middle-income earner.

Day set his sights on this neglected middle-class market. Using his planning expertise and Tom Fuqua's sound building background, Cecil created "budget-luxury" apartments throughout the city.

"Budget-luxury" offered attractive, clean, staggered rows of traditional buildings with large rooms. The high number of units per acre and the creative utility of land combined to make them affordable for a middle-income person. Most of these one-, two- and three-bedroom apartments were close to swimming pools, tennis courts and a clubhouse.

Cecil Day invested in other ventures as well. He bought ten Carrol's Drive-In restaurants from the courthouse steps in Augusta for a fraction of their appraised value. He also acquired several Jiffy's Drive-Ins as a franchisee. Both chains had seen their heydays. To the outsider it looked as though Cecil Day had made a tremendous blunder in picking up businesses that promised only losses.

Cecil Day, however, was interested more in the value of their real estate than in the profit on hamburgers. As his friends and advisors predicted, food sales dwindled, but the real estate value kept creeping up. Day leased the buildings to other entrepreneurs. The structures became laundromats or took on names of other food chains. Everyone was a winner—especially Cecil Day.

In 1969, Cecil sold his holdings to Phipps Land Company for 14 million dollars. That was the largest single real estate transaction in Georgia's history.

With eight million dollars profit in the bank, Cecil could have mapped out his retirement at the ripe old age of 35. That may have been in the back of his mind as he loaded his wife and five children into the family station wagon and headed for an all-summer vacation to California, Canada and Mexico.

Although he was wealthier than 99.9 percent of the nation's population, Cecil grumbled every night during the trip about the high cost of lodging, food and gasoline. He booked rooms at modest motels, bought the least expensive gasoline, and ate only reasonably priced food. Less than three weeks after the day he left, Cecil Day was back in Atlanta.

"Cecil!" shouted a friend when he saw Day walk down the hall of his office building. "I thought you were going to take a vacation and enjoy retirement."

"I'm still on vacation," said Day. "But. . . . "

"But, what?" asked his friend.

"I've got another idea," said Cecil.

3

Look for Things
That Won't Work

Cecil Day would always figure out a way to do something when everyone else was stumped.

—Joe W. Rogers, Jr.
President, Waffle House

The Day brothers, Lon and Cecil, stand before the second Day Building. They worked together in the restaurant, apartment and real estate businesses. Today, Lon carries on the proud Day tradition in real estate as chairman of Day Realty of Atlanta.

When you follow a dream that comes from your heart, when you listen and stay true to the Holy Spirit directing your steps, you're never alone.

—Cecil B. Day

Frost painted web-like patterns on car windshields that January morning of 1970. Cecil Day had just finished his calisthenics with a few friends at the YMCA, when they began their three-times-a-week ritual of jogging.

Day ran alongside one of his friends. They sped up slightly to the head of the pack, then far enough ahead of it so they could talk without being overheard.

"Cecil, let me get this straight," jabbered his friend, who was bouncing along beside him. "You're proposing to build a 'no-name' motel on a 'no-name island'?"

"Yep," abruptly answered Day, continuing his steady gait. "I like Tybee Island."

"But Cecil," his friend continued, "every major motel and hotel chain has denied you a franchise there."

"I know," Day shot back, smiling. "But I still have a vacant piece of dirt down on Tybee that isn't doing anything but cost me money in taxes and interest."

"Big deal—Tybee Island, Georgia," his friend continued. "What do you expect Tybee to become? The new Disneyland of Georgia?"

Day said nothing, but kept jogging, smiling, and looking straight ahead, while his friend softly chuckled at his own last remark.

"Cecil," continued his friend, "I'm talking to you as a friend. You don't even *know* the motel business. What, in heaven's name, are you doing? The experts who know the area have already told you, 'No dice. It won't work. Forget it!' "

Cecil remained undaunted. "If I listened to all the so-called 'experts,' I'd be afraid to get out of my house and drive a car."

"But don't statistics mean anything to you at all?" lamented his friend, whose cheeks now had turned a deep red.

"Sure they do," admitted Cecil, never breaking his stride, "but statistics are not always right." He paused in his speaking to emphasize his point. "Let me put it this way. How much longer than me have you been jogging four miles at a time?"

"Ah . . . . I began about five years before you," puffed his friend. "Why?"

"Well," smiled Day, looking over at his friend, "your breathing is very heavy. What's wrong? Out of breath already?"

Cecil leaned his head forward into the wind. It whistled past his ears as he sprinted the last 100 yards, leaving his friend behind, too breathless to respond.

This wasn't the first time someone shrugged his shoulders at Day's unorthodox ideas. Some doubted him when he started out as Cecil B. Day, Broker. Their doubts were not unfounded. Cecil swallowed more dust than he sold in that first real estate endeavor. Following that failure, he joined Deen's uncles in the heating and air-conditioning business. But his heart remained with real estate. When he did return to real estate by joining the Scott Hudgens Company, even his closest friends doubted his ability to succeed in the profession in which he previously failed.

Many accused him of pipe dreaming when he bought into the Jiffy's and Carrol's food franchises—two fast-food businesses that were in a steep nosedive. Although Day did what he could to level out those operations, they crashed! Rather than throw his hands in the air and walk away from those financially doomed hamburger chains, Cecil Day tried something different.

When he bought into the Jiffy's and Carrol's fast-food businesses, other investors had no interest in them; in fact, his was the only hand raised as the auctioneer pounded the gavel. But Cecil Day saw something in these properties that those others could not. Several weeks prior to the auction, he personally inspected the restaurants and the property surrounding them for their real estate potential.

The restaurants themselves were designed for failure. Prominent "FOR SALE" signs drew more attention than the ones identifying the businesses. Paper and other debris blew across empty parking lots. Faded red and white paint on the Carrol's exterior suggested its product was second-rate.

Some of these properties were surrounded by undesirable amenities—slow growth, no growth or overbuilt locales.

But Cecil Day looked beyond the obvious.

On vacant land, where scraggly trees abounded, many people saw only the dead oaks. Cecil envisioned shopping malls that would one day replace withered leaves. A shopping mall meant increased traffic past the hamburger shops. That translated into increased sales and greater profits.

Potential profits were not the only reasons for purchasing a hamburger chain from the courthouse steps, and Day knew that. He also looked for some degree of financial safety.

If the cash register ceased ringing, he still had the building and real estate on which it sat. The building could house other businesses—some of which could become even more profitable enterprises than the one selling hamburgers.

If all else failed, Day could remain patient and stick with proven formula he learned from Scott Hudgens: Generate cash from a property while it escalated in real estate value, then sell it.

Fast-food restaurants created cash flow, but not enough for Cecil to keep them as viable businesses. So he sold properties at a time when they peaked in value, for a profit that would make Donald Trump proud. The bottom line was that he turned what others considered only a rotten batch of burgers into a real estate success.

Listening to the Holy Spirit

"Many people consider me a loner," Cecil once said. "They may be right to an extent. But when you're following a dream that comes from your heart, when you listen and stay true to the Holy Spirit directing your steps, you're never alone. It's then you begin to walk. When you learn to walk, you begin to look with an 'investor's eye.' It's at that time you see things in a different light."

While Cecil sensed that he was moving toward something previously unseen, his blind faith in his projects and in himself clashed with logic. The conversation while jogging with his friend haunted him. He tried coming up with sound answers to all the "whys" of venturing out. As hard as he tried, he could not. The odds stacked heavily against him as he weighed the upside and downside of the risks he chose to take. Logic told him to forget his dreams; statistics echoed the warning.

But these were the moments when Cecil Day was at his best. He delighted in looking for things that others claimed would not work. When others turned away from some unchartered venture, he kept walking.

His decisions to keep going affected not just him but eventually millions of people throughout the world.

The amazing truth about all this is that his daring approach to business and life didn't involve any revolutionary new idea. By simply stopping, looking and listening, he was able to see things that others missed or took for granted.

Day had earned a sizable profit when he sold a large number of apartments in 1969—at the same time Walt Disney World was preparing to open in Orlando, Florida.

During the next two years, Day often drove the interstates from Atlanta to Orlando. Construction was not completed on the interstates. Travelers were often detoured off the main highway onto blacktop roads where speed limits were low.

Most people cursed the detour signs. Day, on the other hand, saw them as previews of coming attractions. Those signs spelled out in bold terms, through unseen letters, that potentially valuable real estate was not far away.

Others saw only red stop signs; Cecil Day saw green dollar signs.

Southern Gentleman Diplomacy

Realizing the potential of the property was one thing; buying it was another. Most of the property in South Georgia had been owned by southerners for generations. Most of these owners were reluctant to sell to anyone who wasn't "local."

One day, while Cecil was taking a personal survey of some of that farmland, a shotgun blast shook the air. Cecil turned abruptly toward the farmhouse. A man in a three-piece suit, wide-eyed, briefcase in hand, was running away from the old clapboard shack.

A scrawny, little man in his late '70s stood on the front porch of the shack, shaking a clenched fist high over his head. Smoke billowed out of the gun barrel. "Don't you eva come back agin, or I'll git ya where it hurts next time!" he shouted.

Running past Cecil, the salesman hollered in a frightened voice, "Get outta here. That old man's crazy!"

BOOM! Another shot was fired—this one about ten feet over Cecil's head.

"You, too!" yelled the owner.

Cecil obliged and quickly followed the salesman in a swift exit from the farm. Cecil finally caught up with the salesman who had already entered his car bearing a New York license tag.

"Wait a minute," Cecil panted, leaning on the door of the salesman's shiny new Lincoln. "I'd like to talk with you."

Day calmed the salesman's battered nerves and invited him to meet for a cup of coffee at a Waffle House two miles away. Their meeting was brief, but Cecil learned a lot from the discussion.

"For the last two months," said the salesman, with a thick Brooklyn accent. "I've been trying to get that old man to sell his property. I've offered him a bundle for that land, but he won't take *anything* for it."

"Why?" asked Cecil, sipping his coffee.

"Beats me," answered the salesman. "Has something to do with my being a northerner, I suppose. He called me a 'no good yankee.' "

Cecil laughed politely. "Now you know how it feels to be called a 'redneck,' " Cecil said.

"That's what I called the old man. I thought it was proper," argued the salesman.

"Well," said Cecil, "that was your first mistake."

"Calling him a redneck?" asked the salesman.

"Probably more important was *how* you called him that," responded Cecil.

The salesman became irritated at listening to advice given by some local stranger.

"I'm getting out of here," he said, as he rose from the table and brushed dust from his jacket. "Youse guys can have each other."

Cecil paid for the coffee, then drove home. He wanted that property. But how could he convince the old man to sell? He played over and over in his mind the events of that afternoon, searching for the missing piece that would solve the puzzle.

The next day he returned to the property and the home of the old man who, just 24 hours earlier, had fired a warning shot over his head. This time, Cecil was not wearing his usual starched white shirt and tie; instead, he wore a brown flannel shirt and corduroy pants.

Cecil paused long enough to read the man's name scribbled on a rotting wood mailbox that tilted on a homemade post. His shoes left marks in the gravel and red dirt driveway as he headed for the house.

A squeaky screen door suddenly slammed shut.

Cecil didn't jump or act surprised. Instead, he leaned over, picked up a stone and carefully aimed it at a tree 30 feet away. Winding his arm like a baseball pitcher ready to throw a strike, he leaned forward and hurled the stone as hard as he could. When he heard a resounding "THUD!" he hollered, "Bulls-eye!"

Cecil then saw the old man staring at him. A shotgun lay across the farmer's lap as he slowly rocked in a chair. The wrinkle-faced man shifted a yellow baseball cap on his head and continued casting a suspicious leer at Day. He said nothing, while puffing steadily on a pipe.

"How ya doin', Mr. Johnson?" asked Cecil.

"Fine," snapped the farmer, raising the shotgun barrel toward the roof. "How *you* doin', and watcha want?"

"Your permission."

"Permission? Fur whut?"

"To sit down in that chair next to you."

The old man eyed Cecil's hefty, six-foot frame, then thumped the empty chair approvingly.

Day sat down and rocked in the chair. "How long you been raising peanuts?" Cecil pointed to the orderly rows of green tops on each side of the driveway.

The old man stopped puffing his pipe. "How'd you know they was peanuts?" he asked.

" 'Cause I grew up in these parts—more southeast, though. Near Savannah," replied Cecil matter-of-factly.

"Been growin 'em about twenty years. Why?"

"Just askin'," Cecil said.

The old man continued rocking, while puffing on his pipe. Looking to the roof for the right words to fill the less-than-exciting discussion, Cecil blurted, "My dad used to preach all over this part of the state."

The old man stopped rocking.

"What's the name?"

"I'm Cecil Day," he said, extending his hand, which the old man ignored.

"Not you, son," said the old man, now leaning closer. "Your daddy. What's *his* name?"

"Day—Reverend Lon Day," Cecil said, not knowing what to expect.

The old man's eyes lit up like flashbulbs.

"I knowed him!" the old man said with excitement in his voice. "He used ta preach in my church a-ways down th' road years back."

"Can't say I'm shocked," Cecil said.

"Yeah, buddy," laughed the old man. "He could preach th' devil right outta hell."

The two talked at length. Soon, the old man wanted to

know more about Cecil. Day told him of his real estate business and complimented the man on owning such a fine piece of land. "If you ever want to sell your property," Cecil said, "I'd like to buy it."

Before he left the now jovial farmer, Cecil placed a business card in his calloused hand. "Call me if I can help you," Cecil said before returning to his car.

One year later, Cecil bought the old man's land. Although many businessmen wanted it, a genuine down-to-earth admiration of Cecil's demeanor played a key factor in the farmer's decision to sell it to someone who *knocked politely* at his door, rather than *pounding* it.

Cecil Day had, indeed, found the missing piece of the puzzle.

Fulfilling the Tybee Dream

At first, Day thought he would buy more land along the interstates, then wait for them to escalate in value. That's what Scott Hudgens taught him to do in Atlanta. That was the safe wager. Interstate property—especially at intersections—were sound locations that would be valuable once the expressways linked together without detours.

It was the logical approach, certainly. Yet Day was still a developer at heart. He longed for the smell of sawdust. He missed the sounds of hammers banging on rooftops and the shrills of sawblades cutting lumber for wall partitions.

Sitting in the quiet isolation of his home office, he pulled out an old roll of drafting paper and tacked a piece onto his drafting table—a relic from his days at Georgia Tech. Using some tattered blueprints of the "budget-luxury" apartments he once built, Cecil sketched some new concepts for a motel on Tybee Island.

The next day he met with his builder-friend, Tom Fuqua, and discussed details about the new building.

"How soon can you start building this motel?" he asked.

"Tomorrow, I guess," Tom replied, not knowing if Day was serious in his question.

Cecil was.

That very night, Fuqua made telephone calls from his home. He solicited subcontractors until two in the morning to make the six-hour drive with him to Tybee. Shortly after sunset the next day, Fuqua and his building crew crossed the last high bridge that connects Savannah with Tybee Island.

Tybee Island—four miles long and two miles wide—has one red light, a tiny post office run by one person and a small brick city hall. It's quiet. Sometimes it is difficult to tell which is louder—the flapping of the large American flag near city hall or the pounding waves of the Atlantic on the beaches of fine, tan sand.

About 2,400 people live here all year; hundreds of thousands of tourists' footprints are left in the sand each spring and summer.

In the 1920s, especially during Prohibition, Tybee enjoyed its heyday. It was the period when big bands—Tommy Dorsey, Glenn Miller and Sammy Kaye—came here to entertain "flappers" who danced to the beat of drums and waves on a pavilion that extended over the ocean. Wealthy men wore white suits and Panama hats. They spoke openly of big money, while sophisticated ladies swam in the salty waters in pantaloon-like swimwear.

Slot machines dotted the island. A one-armed bandit was the center of attraction even at the local post office, before the Federal Government ordered it ripped off the walls.

After World War II, however, Tybee losts its big-name image. Many of its magnificent ocean homes fell into disrepair. The tourist industry slacked off over the next two decades. Even the island's once grand monument—the Tybee Hotel— was torn down in 1960, a victim of the slumping tourist trade that had dropped off to nearly zero. A few years later, a fire, driven by winds zipping across the Atlantic, destroyed the pavilion where people once danced and roller-skated. The fire also destroyed most of Tybee's amusement attractions. By 1961, less than a dozen family-owned motels competed for the few tourists who happened to come by.

That's when Cecil Day bought a small portion of land where the once majestic Tybee Hotel stood. Chunks of her concrete still remained on the ground—a sad commentary on a proud, fallen structure.

Cecil never knew exactly why he bought the small lot, except that he loved the island's relaxing atmosphere. To him, the purchase just "felt right."

Like Jiffy's and Carrol's, Tybee Island was another example of an enterprise that had seen its glory days. But Cecil built a motel there in 1970, in spite of the counsel from well-meaning friends. His first innkeepers were his mother and an established motel wizard from Tybee— George Spirades.

As the official opening day neared, maid service was impossible to find; so Cecil paid his own children to make up beds. His wife ripped open the plastic of new pillows and put cases on them. As soon as a room was cleaned, Cecil called the front desk and gave the signal to rent it.

The weight of a truck delivering motel furniture was too great for the bridge to the island. Consequently, Cecil's mother made regular trips in her station wagon to the truck parked on the mainland for necessary furnishings.

By April, only a few months after a friend ribbed Cecil about building a "no-name motel on a no-name island," all 60 rooms of this Tybee Island property were filled.

The motel enjoyed 100 percent occupancy most of the summer, but Cecil refused to place a "NO VACANCY" sign outside. He wanted people to come in and enjoy his mother's home-spun hospitality; that would entice them to return.

There was no time for any ribbon-cutting ceremony. Instead, Cecil and Tom Fuqua just relaxed and watched tourists line up to pay eight dollars for a night's lodging. But the silent celebration lasted no more than a few minutes.

"Tom," asked Cecil, still smiling, "remember that piece of real estate I bought near I-75 in Forsyth?"

"Yeah," sighed Tom, still beaming. "When can I begin?"

4

Identify What's Really Important

Cecil B. Day demonstrated by example that a rich family life and professional success can be achieved based on biblical principles.

—Jimmy Carter

In addressing a group of realtors, Cecil stresses the importance of applying Judeo-Christian ethics in business.

You don't have to be a CEO to start Christian activities in a business.

—Cecil B. Day

Fewer things reveal the secret of Cecil Day's success than his ability to identify what was really important.

Were you to ask any businessman what was important to the success of his ventures, his first response probably would be: "To earn a profit."

On the surface, that makes sense. Without showing a profit, the company would cease to exist. But Cecil was convinced that profit could not be the only criterion for success. Other values far outweighed this.

The amazing result was that by establishing other priorities and sticking with them, Cecil Day was able to enjoy even more profits than he ever thought possible—even during hard times.

Five important dimensions ruled Cecil Day's approach to business. While they may not be the same as those taught at fashionable business schools, few can argue the fact that they worked.

1. God and His Church

One theme ran thoughout the life and work of Cecil Day: "I must serve God and His church."

By the term "church," Cecil was willing to look beyond the four walls of a particular building. His home congregation and Southern Baptist denomination were important to him, but these weren't the limits of God's church. To Cecil, the church included other denominations and various missionary efforts—especially the Haggai Institute with headquarters in Atlanta. Cecil supported the work of this organization, which he felt offered "the most logical solution to the quest of winning the world to Christ by training third world nationals so they can teach their own people, in their own language, without superimposing Western culture on the Gospel."

Not everyone in the corporation completely understood Cecil Day's concept of priorities, especially when it involved God and His church. Four years after Day's death in 1978, then Days Inns CEO, Richard Kessler (now no longer with the firm), declared to an Atlanta newspaper reporter: "Sometimes, the fact that we run this corporation based on Christian ethics is miscommunicated. We are not a church. We are a business and we are in business to earn a fair and equitable profit."

Cecil Day would have taken great exception to the spirit of Kessler's personal assessment of Days Inns' new business mentality. While both Day and Kessler would have agreed that a business should operate profitably, Day would have contended that business—at least *his* business—was most definitely church-like.

Like a church, Days Inns were service-oriented. Each motel was operated in such a way that it served the interests of the customers in ways that were unique to the motel business.

Like a church, the motels had no bars and sold no alcoholic beverages. Day stood by this conviction in spite of numerous protests from some bankers and others concerned only with bottom line profits.

Like a church, each motel offered pastoral services. A "Chaplain on Call" card was prominently displayed in every Days Inns room. Day paid a staff to set up, monitor and maintain a network of chaplains as a ministry for each motel. The concept paid off. Many times local ministers, priests and rabbis were called by distraught guests. Hundreds of marriages were saved as were the lives of those who contemplated suicide. When necessary, chaplains were available to counsel employees with personal problems.

This was not a new concept to Cecil Day. His convictions took root during his mid-twenties. It was a time when Day was confused about what God wanted him to do with his life. Often he thought God was calling him to be a minister like his father. He met with his pastor, Dr. Solomon Dowis, every Thursday morning for about a year as he wrestled with the situation. Together, the two of them knelt in prayer asking for God's guidance. Finally, the answer pierced Day's heart: Remain a Christian businessman, and from business you'll have a ministry.

Day stayed in business and succeeded. In response to his unique calling to serve the Lord through business, Day set up a foundation to help struggling churches. Many churches, Day noticed, were not affiliated with a particular denomination that funded mission efforts. Day's foundation helped fill this void.

Ten percent of Day Realty's profits were placed into this small foundation. Day selected a few church members, business associates and family members to serve on a committee as trustees.

As Day's success grew, so did the foundation. When Days Inns evolved out of Day Realty, it, too, tithed ten percent of its profits into the foundation. That ten percent was divided in line with the faith of the stockholders. "Our major stockholders are not of the same faith," Day said. "We allocate an approximate amount, according to how much stock the stockholder holds." If, for example, 50 percent of the stockholders were Baptist, 20 percent were Lutheran, and 27 percent Roman Catholic, and 3 percent Jewish, the monies would be allocated to churches and synagogues accordingly.

Outsiders learned of Day's foundation. Requests for help most often came from people he had never met. One handwritten letter was typical of the ones that impressed him:

> Dear Mr. Day:
>
> I know that you are a very busy man, but I am experiencing some problems and don't know exactly what to do. With all my might, I've tried earning extra money working extra jobs between preaching at my church to cover my terminally ill daughter's medical expenses. I've been able to make ends meet until recently.
>
> My seven-year-old automobile blew a transmission. The lowest estimate I have (enclosed) is $376.78. If you can help me on this, I promise to pay you back. If you can't help me, I'll understand.

Cecil immediately sent the writer a check along with a letter of encouragement. One year later, the money was paid in full with a "thank you" note from the borrower.

Cecil did more for the foundation than sit in an air-conditioned office reviewing requests. Even while taking family vacations, he stopped at each of the churches he supported to see how his funds were appropriated. Often he and his family worshipped in small, New England churches made of unpainted concrete walls, and sat on pews made of 2" x 12" boards propped up by bricks and blocks.

One pastor remarked, "Cecil's visits were as important as his financial support. I never expected a financier to take time to visit and encourage me."

In 1976, Days Inns were still reeling from the Arab oil embargo. When it looked as though this crisis was coming to an end, Day called together his financial staff, along with representatives of the foundation. "I want you to give me a fiscal projection for next year," he told his financial staff. "I want to know what profits you anticipate showing at the end of that year."

Day then turned to the foundation representatives. "Once they get their numbers, I'll start tithing ten percent of the projected income immediately—*before* the projected income is earned."

The representatives nodded their heads. They were amazed at Cecil's pledge, but not surprised. Unlike some of his closest business associates, they knew that the number one priority of Day's life and work was serving God and His church.

2. Creditors

The 727 Eastern Airlines jet began its slow descent into a midwestern city. Cecil Day could see from 6,000 feet several sites for new Days Inns. But his trip wasn't to search for new locations. It was to see a franchisee who owed Cecil several thousand dollars.

Frank (not his real name)—a tall, slenderly built, tanned man wearing a black suit with a red silk tie—stood waiting for him at the main gate. He laughed and joked with an attractive blond-haired young woman clinging to his arm.

"Cecil!" Frank shouted as soon as he saw him. "I'm glad you're here safely," he said, while shaking his hand firmly. "By the way, this is my new, overpaid secretary, Wanda," he said with a chuckle.

The three of them walked to the parking lot and got into the franchisee's new Mercedes.

"Ain't she a beaut?" asked Frank.

"Nice car," remarked Cecil. "It still has that 'new' smell."

"That's 'cause it is new," bragged Frank as he cranked up the engine.

"Your motel is near here, isn't it?" Cecil asked.

"Yeah, but before I take you there, I'd like to drive you around and show you a few things."

Frank exited the expressway onto a road lined with trees. "See that building up on that hill?" asked Frank, pointing to an old Tudor-style building. Ivy-covered walls added warmth to its rust-colored bricks.

"That's where my two children go to school," said Frank. "It costs a fortune to send them there; but it's worth it. That school has one of the best tutoring programs in the area."

Frank sped up his car. A few miles down the road he turned left into a subdivision with an impressive flagstone entrance that surrounded a cast iron gate opened by a security guard who called Frank by name.

"This is my neighborhood," said Frank. "My house is right around this corner."

The three-story Victorian house sat atop a grassy knoll. A well-manicured lawn was the pride of the gardner who was busy cutting rows of boxwood hedges near the front of the house.

"Some house, huh Cecil?"

"It's nice, all right." Cecil paused. "Good grief! How many square feet does that thing have?"

"About 6,000, not including the servant's quarters," beamed Frank. "But I bet your house puts this one to shame, Cecil."

"Hardly. My house has 2,400 square feet, and all seven of my family live in it comfortably," Cecil replied without apology.

They continued driving to the motel. What Cecil saw

after they arrived did not make him happy at all. The parking lot was only half full. Litter blew across the asphalt. A hose dangled from a pump on the gasoline island and blew in the wind.

"We've been doing pretty good here, Cecil, everything considered," said Frank.

"I know," said Cecil. "Last week you averaged 73 percent occupancy. You're doing better than most of us. Some locations are lucky to get 50 percent these days."

The two left the secretary in the Mercedes and went inside the Tasty World restaurant.

"Things look like they're going great guns for you," Cecil said. "So, I guess you'll be able to begin repaying me that money you owe me. I can use it right now."

Frank broke eye contact with Cecil and slumped his shoulders. His face sagged dismally. "Cecil . . . I . . . ah . . . don't have it right now. You know how it is with house payments, tuition, salaries and all that. My divorce is still pending, and the attorney fees are eating me alive."

Day's face turned a slight shade of red. He rose from the table, walked away a few steps, took a deep breath, then returned, looking Frank squarely in the eye. He spoke in a hushed but sturdy voice that showed the seriousness of what he said. "I do expect you to pay me back exactly the way you promised me you would."

"But Cecil, you're a Christian businessman!" Frank blurted out. "Certainly you can understand my predicament."

"My Christianity has nothing to do with the debt-service you've acquired," said Cecil in that same hushed voice. "I still have a business to run, bills to pay and a family to feed. As a matter of fact, at my house we've cut back on our spending because we can't afford buying what we could before. Bankers and vendors knock at my door each day expecting me to pay them as you promised to pay me. And, as far as my Christianity goes, I'd be a bald-faced liar to any lender I failed to diligently repay, regardless of my situation.

"Cecil," Frank laughed, "you surprise me. I've always been told that Christians were to be meek."

"There's a big difference between 'meek' and 'weak,'" Cecil stammered, his voice now showing effects of emotion. "I expect your first payment on Monday."

Frank wasn't the first man to challenge Cecil Day's patience regarding payment of bills. Cecil had no reservations about confronting people who owed him money. Just as it was important to him to pay bills on time, he expected the same from others.

Cecil called it an application of the Golden Rule. "I have always tried living up to my promises," he later recalled. "Frank made a promise to me, and we signed a document to that effect. So how do I want to be treated in this situation? I want to be paid on time—in the same way I repay others."

Based upon the lessons he learned from real world experience with others who were slow in paying debts, Cecil Day created what many business people consider the most pragmatic formula to offer those who owe you money:

1. If you owe me money, come and see me if you cannot pay me right now. Don't hide.

2. Acknowledge the debt and agree on the amount to be paid.

3. Tell me how you plan to pay the debt. It may be in 12, 24 or 36 payments. That may not be what I want to hear because I need my money right now. But pay me a little now and give me your plan to pay the balance.

4. Be a person of your word. Deliver what you promise. I've been able to do this 95 percent of the time. Although it was embarrassing for me to have to do this, it helped me establish trust and credibility with those to whom I owed money.

3. Employees

Cecil Day didn't hire employees; he adopted them. Certainly, he did the normal things associated with good managment-labor relations. He published an employee newsletter— called *Days World*—that informed the workers as to goals and strategies of the Days Inns of America, Inc. He talked with employees on a one-to-one basis. He gave a pat on the back to the employee who went an extra mile.

On occasion, some financial people on Day's staff advised him to get rid of secretaries who were drawing high salaries because of long service and replace them with new hires who would not demand as much money.

"Not on your life," said Cecil. "These employees have been faithful to me; I'll be faithful to them. Besides, they have things the new employee would never have—experience and knowledge about our business, not to mention loyalty."

Whether or not that made good business sense according to modern textbooks was of no concern to Cecil Day. Outside of God, his church, his family and the obligation he owed to creditors, he held his employees in highest regard.

Day demonstrated that dedication to his employees in the most significant way he could imagine. He shared with them the opportunity to meet the Lord who was in charge of his life.

Cecil Day never tried to cram down the throats of his employees any particular denominational teaching; rather he attempted to lead by example those who would want to know his Master.

Day initiated into his corporation a unique program of weekly devotionals. These Tuesday morning gatherings, which lasted 45 minutes, were quite informal, although each included prayers, readings from the Bible, and often a presentation by an invited speaker.

Day emphasized that when it came to his employees,

he was willing to deal with the whole person—physical, mental and spiritual.

His idea caught fire. Up to 50 percent of the employees attended these weekly devotionals that began one hour before regular work hours, although there was never any hint of pressure from headquarters to attend.

Until then, no other major corporation in the Atlanta area would even consider such a thing. "It might cause problems," cautioned one plant manager. But other executives with whom Day dealt in his business saw the value in the devotionals. His former boss, Scott Hudgens, offered the same program for employees in his company. Even some of the banks that worked with Day followed suit. They, too, held similar devotions each week.

Not only did the employees appreciate this opportunity to worship with each other, they also enjoyed other benefits from attending the devotionals. Coworkers became more unified. A cooperative spirit carried through the entire week. Tension, gossip, jealousy—all were reduced; obviously people couldn't pray together one minute, then stab others in the back the next.

Some of the employees who left Days Inns for one reason or another carried with them the idea for other companies to include devotionals in their weekly programs. Cecil Day often remarked, "You don't have to be a CEO to start Christian activities in a business."

4. Family

One of the expected standards of behavior for today's business executive is to place on his or her desk photographs of spouse and children. Obviously, the purpose of this display is to tell the world—at least those who visit the office—that the executive in question deems family important.

Cecil Day may have had photos of his family on his desk, but he didn't need to do so. Everyone who knew anything about Day knew of his devotion to his wife and five children.

In fact, far more important than earning a dollar was the welfare of his family.

Cecil Day even had a sixth sense about this.

In 1975, at the Day home in Atlanta, Cecil's eldest son and his fiancee were making final preparations for their wedding scheduled just one week away. But something was wrong. Instead of glowing with anticipation, the couple realized it just wouldn't work out.

Reluctantly, at four that afternoon, both of them told Deen Day about their decision to call the whole thing off.

The family was suddenly thrown into a turmoil. Something must be done quickly about scheduled parties, wedding gifts and floral arrangements. Telephone calls must be made to relatives . . . friends . . . the church. . . .

At that precise moment, Cecil Day had just driven a rental car out of a parking lot at the Los Angeles airport. In less than one hour he would be inspecting some of the hottest property in L.A. as a site for a new motel.

But something didn't feel right. His stomach felt cold. That happened on more than one occasion. Through some uncanny—some called it "intuition"—feeling, Cecil sensed when something was wrong at home. It happened, for example, when one of the children accidently poked Deen in the eye with the edge of a book. Deen grabbed her eye in pain. There appeared to be no permanent damage, but she had nowhere to turn for help.

Cecil was driving to a business meeting out of Atlanta and felt that unmistakable chill in his stomach. He turned the car 180 degrees and headed for home immediately.

This day, in Los Angeles, Day quickly turned the car back toward the airport. He drove to the luggage check-in area, threw his keys under the seat, and walked quickly toward the ticket counter.

"Hey!" bellowed a baggage clerk. "You can't park here, mister!"

Day continued walking away.

"Hey, you! Come back here!"

Ignoring the baggage clerk, Day walked to the airline counter. "When's the next flight to Atlanta?" he asked the gate agent.

"We have a flight that leaves in two hours, ten minutes," the agent replied with a smile.

"What about other airlines?" asked Cecil.

The agent looked at the computer screen. "Delta has one leaving in fifteen minutes. They have one seat available. But I doubt you'll have time to make. . . ."

"Book me on it right away," interrupted Day.

"I'll let them know you're coming," said the agent.

Holding tightly to his suitcase, Day quickly wove his way through the mass of passengers at the LAX terminal. Delta flights left from another concourse. In exactly 14 minutes he was at the gate for the Delta flight. He was too late. The ramp had already been pulled away from the aircraft.

"I must get on that flight," Day demanded.

"Well . . . I . . . the ramp is . . . ," stammered the gate agent.

"I don't care what it takes. I must get on that plane. Please let me on."

The urgency of Day's plea worked. The agent quickly grabbed her walkie-talkie and notified the pilot. The ramp was moved back to the aircraft, and Cecil boarded.

"Thanks a lot!" shouted Day as he waved to the gate attendant.

Sitting in the only empty seat of the plane, Cecil thought to himself: "What in the world am I doing? I broke a meeting for some crazy impulse. Right now I should be looking at the best location for a Days Inns, and soon I'll be 31,000 feet in the sky."

Four hours later, the plane landed at Hartsfield International Airport in Atlanta. By nine that night, Day was in the living room of his home consoling his wife and son.

"I'm proud of you, son," said Cecil.

His son looked bewildered. This wasn't a very proud moment for him. "Proud of me? Why?"

"For making a tough decision and sticking to what you feel is right."

"Dad," his son's voice quivered with emotion, "if I've ever seen an angel, it would have been you tonight."

The next morning, Day called his secretary. "Jo, cancel all my appointments today. I need to spend time with one of my children."

Cecil Day discussed the impulse to fly home only with those very close to him. He called it his "invisible hand." Others marveled at his gift for sensing something "unforeseen"; to Day it was like the string being tugged by a kite in the sky as described by his father.

By whatever name we call it, the pulling power showed the importance of family to Cecil Day.

And that says a lot more than do photos on top of a desk.

5. The "Last Man"

Fewer things grieved Cecil Day more than budget cuts—especially if it meant trimming payroll. He felt a special obligation ⸜ his employees. Cuts in pay affected families of those he had grown to love.

Not many realized, however, that whenever the time came to trim back the payroll, Cecil Day started with his own.

John Haggai, founder of the famed Haggai Institute, recalls one example:

> The oil embargo nearly sank his motel empire. Yet it was here that Cecil's determination to follow through on his commitments really came into its own. Immediately, he cut his salary to $100 a week, explaining his points and his proposed solutions. Meanwhile, his family lived in Spartan conditions.

"The hardest thing," Cecil told me, *"is to set your goal and stick to it."*

Cecil Day's success was no accident. His willingness to pay others before he paid himself was, in no small way, responsible for the solid reputation he earned in the business world.

Bankers willingly gave credit to him while denying others with just as much capital.

Employees for Days Inns of America worked longer hours and over many years, while workers at other corporations formed unions and talked of strikes.

Day's approach to business said, in effect, "All of you are important to me. And I am willing to serve you before myself. I am the 'last man' on the ladder of importance."

Determining what was important worked for Cecil Day.

5

Mold a Sense of Values

> *Cecil B. Day was an extremely successful businessman who never compromised his religious values for the sake of career gain.*
>
> —Andrew Young

Day answers a question posed by Pat Robertson, host of the internationally televised "700 Club."

> *I am convinced that you don't have to compromise a sense of values just to make money.*
>
> —Cecil B. Day

Springtime in Forsyth, Georgia is an artist's dream. Saturday, April 4, 1970, was no exception. Tourists traveling I-75 between Macon and Atlanta swelled the city of 3,600 residents as they did each year around this time.

An unusually bright sun made the flowering shrubs stand out against a background of well-manicured lawns. Students from historic Tift College returning from a one-week Easter vacation added their appreciative "oohs" and "ahhhs" to the first signs of spring.

Cecil Day was also attracted to the budding colors in Forsyth that afternoon, but not those of flowers, trees or any gifts of nature. The only colors he thought about all day were the green and gold of the city's Holiday Inn sign two miles south of where he was standing.

With an associate, Fred, Day had just completed a personal inspection of a vacant lot along the east side of busy Interstate 75, near the northern edge of Forsyth. He was oblivious to the condition of his shoes from the hour's walk through the muddy field.

"Those folks do great business," he said, pointing in the direction of the Holiday Inn.

"They sure do," agreed Fred, who had accompanied him on the 60-mile trip south of Atlanta. "It's a terrific location. I understand they had more than 70 percent occupancy last year."

"I wonder if we could do even better?" Cecil asked with a smile.

"What do you mean, 'we'?" asked Fred, still unaware of why they made this hour-long trip from Atlanta in the first place.

"Holiday Inn has obviously done the market survey, so they've saved us money there. And they have a great location but this property can be just as good. And it's a lot cheaper than what Holiday Inn paid for their site. It'll work just fine for a new motel. What do you think?"

"Well. . . . "

Cecil didn't wait for his answer. "Fred," he said, "this feels good. As soon as we get back home, get me the details on this property."

Fred did. The price and terms were even better than Day had anticipated. Using part of the money earned from the sale of the apartments, Day bought the property and ordered plans for a new Days Inn to be constructed by fall. With the purchase of the Forsyth property, Cecil Day was no longer the owner of one "no-name motel on a no-name island." Instead, he took his first step in creating a chain of motels.

It may be important to remember what Cecil accomplished in the years that followed; but those closest to him feel that it is far more important to remember *how* he did it all.

The media trumpets stories of business successes, which are often accompanied by steamy accounts of underhanded methods by men and women convinced that the ends always justify the means. The main characters in these tales are people for whom the word "ethics" is a nice ideal, but far removed from the cruel realities of the everyday business world.

Cecil Day was not one of those people.

Day was convinced that you didn't need to compromise your values just to earn a buck. Instead, he was convinced that with a proper code of ethics, he could become more successful than he ever imagined. To support this belief he often quoted one of his favorite passages from the New Testament: "The measure you give will be the measure you get, and still more will be given you" (Mark 4:24).

Cecil Day's values were simple; anyone can understand them. And they were pragmatic; no one can argue with their success. They didn't come from a college textbook, but from years of attendance in the school of hard knocks, together with a lot of common sense.

Day's values can be called "The Belief Pattern":

Business opportunities are all around us.

Expect the best from others.

Loyalty is a two-way street.

Initial reactions are usually best.

Eliminate alcohol.

Faith in God is essential.

Business Opportunities Are All Around Us

"Each day we pass by more opportunities to earn money than we ever dreamed we could face in one lifetime," he told his business partners at a corporate meeting. The sooner-than-expected opening of his Forsyth motel illustrated exactly what he meant.

Before the payment was laid for the parking lot, a typical Georgia summer thunderstorm hurled dime-sized drops of rain on the new property and on everyone within a hundred miles of Forsyth. Water covering the muddy parking lot saturated a makeshift plywood path leading from the sidewalk along the interstate to the motel entrance.

The motel manager, dressed in a pair of blue jeans and a red flannel work shirt, had just patched a small leak in the roof of the newly constructed 120-room motel. He and a skeleton crew had been working overtime, as they had every night that week, in order to get the facility ready for its official opening in exactly seven days. His shoes made tracks in the sawdust and bits of plaster left on the floor by carpenters.

The manager was just about to turn off the lights in the lobby area when he heard a tapping on the glass front door. Outside, about 20 people stood under umbrellas, bracing themselves against a biting wind. One pointed toward the door and gestured to the manager to open it. Tucking in his shirt tail and buttoning the top three buttons of his shirt, the manager unlocked the door. Opening it, he shouted to be heard over the wind by the people outside.

"May I help you?"

"We saw your signs down the interstate . . . you know . . . the ones that say 'Rooms: $8 and up'."

"That's right," the manager agreed, "but we won't be open until a week from now. Come back then. Okay?"

"Can't we stay here anyway?" pleaded a weary-looking man standing next to a tiny woman who was holding her two-year-old daughter, while her older brother tugged rhythmically at her skirt.

"Well . . . just a minute," he said. "I'll be right back."

The manager closed the door, went behind the registration desk to the building's only available telephone and called Cecil Day in Atlanta.

"Mr. Day," said the manager. "You're not goin' to believe this, but there's a bunch of people out here waiting to check in."

"Are you serious?" Day chuckled. "Already?"

"Yes, sir. And I·keep tellin' 'em we won't be opening for a week . . . after the parking lot's paved."

"That's great," said Day.

"Great? What do you mean, 'great'? These people are all muddied-up! And there's this lady with a kid in her arms . . . and one taggin' at her skirt. . . . "

"Well, let them in."

"But, Mr. Day, the beds aren't made up yet . . . and none of the rooms have telephones. . . . Heck, I don't even have a cash register or credit card machine."

"That's okay. Accept checks."

"But what if they bounce?"

"Trust them. What do you have to lose? Besides, I'll worry about that. Look around you. See what you can keep the money in."

The manager put down the phone, looked over the slick countertop, and found something that might serve.

"Mr. Day, all I have is an old nail box with a few nails in it."

"Super. Use it."

"But what about the rooms that haven't been made up yet? The sheets and pillowcases are still wrapped in plastic. I don't have any help. . . . "

"Explain your situation, then ask them if they would put the sheets on the beds themselves."

"Would they do that?"

"Don't know. Let's ask them."

"Okay. I'll give it my best."

The manager opened the door and gave blankets, pillowcases and sheets to the rain-soaked travelers, who happily accepted the challenge of bedding themselves down in the motel.

"No wonder they're only charging eight bucks a night," joked one customer.

Three nights later, all 120 rooms were filled with people. But now it was a lot easier. The manager had a real cash register.

Expect the Best From Others

A skeptic would call him naive. But Cecil Day was not ashamed to admit that he regarded others as being basically good until proved otherwise. When he interviewed potential employees, he sought out those who shared his philosophy and avoided those who thought they were better than others.

"Where did you go to school?" he asked one 23-year-old college graduate.

"Southern Cal. Class of '68," replied the starch-necked job hunter.

"What was your major?"

"I was a 4.0 in economics."

"What do you think of people?"

"Pardon?"

"People . . . what do you think of them?"

"From which perspective, Mr. Day? The social-economic or . . . ?"

"Just people. What do you think of them?"

"Well, given my straight A's in psychology, I learned that. . . . "

"Look, young man, all I want to know is whether you like people."

"That depends on how they treat me."

"How do you like to be treated?"

"With respect."

"Why?"

"Because I worked my tail off at Southern Cal."

"What did you learn about people there?"

"Professors are jerks."

"Why do you say that?"

"They always wanted me to do things their way."

"Good."

"Sir? What do you mean?"

"Those so-called 'jerks' were trying to teach you about the real world, son. And that's something you won't learn in any fancy book."

Cecil Day didn't hire that candidate, but he hired the next interviewee.

"Where did you go to school?"

"Daytona Beach Community College, sir," said the nervous young man.

"What was your major?"

"Economics."

"What do you think of people?"

"Sometimes they can be tough."

"Is it wrong to be tough?"

"No, sir. Tough people have soft spots, too, I guess."

"When can you start working for us?"

"Anytime you want," answered the young man with a grin that filled his face.

"Good. We'll grab a hamburger for lunch this afternoon. I look forward to working with you."

Loyalty Is a Two-way Street

Cecil Day was one of those rare employers who was not surprised that an employee was loyal to him and to the company. He *expected* loyalty. And he knew that loyalty had a way of paying off.

While working for Atlanta developer Scott Hudgens in 1959, Cecil worked extra hours selling property. Annual sales commissions for employees averaged about $8,000—an adequate salary in those days. Cecil earned commissions totaling $50,000. Within just two years, he was offered a promotion to vice president of Hudgens' sprawling real estate empire.

"I learned from Scott Hudgens that by giving a person

space with limited parameters, it challenges the best of their ability and integrity. That usually produces results beyond expectations for both employee and employer."

At the same time, Day firmly believed that loyalty was a two-way street. Some motel owners searched for ways to rid themselves of veteran employees who were costing them too much in salary and benefits, but Cecil Day went out of his way to show his appreciation to his long-time associates. He operated his business with a family-type atmosphere; employees knew he was concerned about them as individuals.

Day's motives were more than altruistic. He realized that it cost time and money to train new employees to work efficiently in the system. Therefore, although seasoned veterans usually are paid more, they're worth every penny.

And the "family" approach to employees resulted in people willing to work for less money. Employees worked hard, long hours, but they did so willingly, with a smile.

During the early days when available cash was poured back into construction projects, the budget showed no allowance for salary increases. Nonetheless, Day let it be known that he appreciated the loyalty of his workers.

Juanita Gargis had been a "utility team player" with the company for two years. Day knew firsthand that she would do anything for Days Inns—including heading the reservations system—often working overtime in order to meet the extra demands of the company's rapid expansion. She is the sort of employee who deserved a show of loyalty. He called her into his office for a conference.

"Juanita," he began, "how long have you been here without a pay raise? Two years?"

"Yes, sir."

"As you know, Juanita, we're putting out a lot of money right now to insure we'll all have jobs next year. . . ."

"I understand," interrupted an empathetic Juanita, who

thought this was merely Day's diplomatic way of telling her she would go another year at the same salary.

". . . But I didn't want you to think I've overlooked you," he continued.

Day reached into the top drawer of his large walnut desk, and pulled out a manila envelope and handed it to her.

Juanita sat, staring puzzle-eyed at her boss.

"Well, go on, open it," Cecil said.

Opening the envelope, she pulled out a personal letter of appreciation from Day.

"How very nice, Mr. Day. Thank you."

"I meant every word of it. There's something else in the envelope, too."

She reached inside and slowly pulled out another sheet of paper. Her eyes filled with tears. "Stock in Days Inns of America!" she exclaimed. "Eight shares. Thank you, Mr. Day," she beamed.

That motel manager in Forsyth who made it possible for tourists to bed down for the night a week before the motel opened also received shares of stock that afternoon. Others were similarly rewarded.

Through these simple but sincere gestures, Day maintained a remarkable staff loyalty. Even his lower-paid employees in high turn-over positions remained with the company for an average of 3.2 years—unheard of in the motel industry.

Initial Reactions Are the Best

In 1968, Bob Williams was a hamburger cook, full-time college student, and manager of a fast food restaurant owned by Cecil Day. Cecil had sized him up as a hardworking, honest man but hadn't seen him since he enlisted in the military.

Two years later, Bob called Cecil to tell him that he had just been discharged from the Army, had completed his college education and was searching for a job. Cecil hired him as his personal assistant.

It was a classic Cecil Day move that ran counter to everything taught at Harvard Business School. Why would anyone select as his personal assistant someone he had not seen for years, and whose previous work experience was unrelated to the job for which he was hired?

Cecil Day's justification was simple: "My gut reaction was to hire him. It felt good to me."

There's more to this story. A month later, Cecil received the horrible news that the superintendent on a construction project of a new motel in Richmond Hill, Georgia, had suddenly quit. Day summoned Bob Williams.

"Bob, I have another task for you," said Day.

"Terrific," said Williams. "Doing what?"

"Supervising the construction of a new motel. What do you think about that?"

The glow left Williams' face. "Build a motel? Cecil, I don't know a rafter from a stud."

"I understand. But will you do it?"

"Sure. When?" asked Williams.

"Now," Cecil replied.

Williams was on the site by nine o'clock that night, learning what had to be done.

Once again, Cecil's gut reaction proved right. Bob Williams wasn't afraid to ask questions. He learned fast. Despite the confusion caused by the supervisor's sudden departure, the project was completed only a few days behind schedule.

Day often reminded his staff, "Sometimes the best way to discover what an employee can do is to throw him in water over his head and see whether he sinks or swims." He pointed to Bob Williams as his prize example.

Eliminate Alcohol

Cecil Day never stood on a soapbox publicly condemning the drinking of alcohol. That was a decision people had to make for themselves. But he vowed he would neither sell nor use alcoholic beverages, even if it meant losing potential business.

That was no empty promise. Day backed his conviction with actions shortly after the plywood became a paved walk at the new motel in Forsyth. Travelers continued to register for the $8-a-night rooms. They also patronized the motel restaurant ("Tasty World Restaurant," Day named it), bought items from the new gift shop and purchased gasoline at the motel's pump—when no other motel chains offered the latter service.

Encouraging news came from the Forsyth motel each day during its first month of operation, demonstrating that budget-conscious travelers were enthusiastic about his concept.

Occupancy far surpassed the 65 percent national average; 95 percent of the 120 rooms were filled each night. Day now dreamed of more motels—14 of them—along the interstates between Georgia and Orlando, Florida, where the new Walt Disney World neared completion.

It was a solid vision. There should be no problem making it work. Day needed only one thing—money!

Dreams plus dreams equal dreams; dreams plus action equal success. It was time to quit dreaming and take action. Enough persuasive data were available to obtain construction loans. It was time to go money-hunting.

Bankers who saw the Forsyth operation were impressed at what Day had done. In spite of this, not one was willing to risk lending money without Day's assurance that his next motels would include bars and lounges. They insisted that this was the only way Day could hope to earn a profit.

"Bars and lounges are expensive to build," Cecil replied. "Insurance rates for the motel with a bar are astronomical. Besides, that's inconsistent with our concept."

"But Cecil, businessmen want bars, especially after traveling. They are the perfect spots for entertaining clients," argued one banker.

"We're not specifically after that market. We're targeting the family."

"I understand, Cecil. But serving drinks can increase your profits in your restaurants as well."

The bankers were right, of course. As any restaurateur knows, there's only a small markup on the food, compared to liquor that can bring at least four times the investment.

"I'm personally against selling alcohol to anyone at any price," Day retorted. "I believe we can build and operate motels successfully without bars. Period."

Cecil Day's convictions about not serving alcohol went beyond deep-rooted religious convictions. He had seen the damage it caused to families, to friendships, to men of great potential, to those who attained their goals only to lose them, even to large corporations. He often told about his boyhood experience with alcohol.

"My family took in a relative who had a drinking problem and put him in the other bed in my small room. Night after night he'd come stumbling in, smelling like the dickens, trying to find his bed, then fall out of it once he found it. After watching him, I knew I'd never drink the stuff."

Building 14 motels was a big project that called for big money. Where does one get big money? In big cities, of course. So Cecil Day visited banks in New York, Chicago and Detroit. But he couldn't raise a dime. Every banker was convinced that a bar was essential to a motel's success; without one, none would make it past the first year.

After three months without success, the frustration was becoming difficult to handle. The usually even-tempered Cecil

Day was showing effects of the stress. No matter what city he was in, the loan committees raised the same objections. In a bank in Chicago, this all came to a head.

"You can't make it without serving alcohol," said one executive.

"Whoever heard of selling gasoline at a motel?" asked another.

"Think of the tired businessman who wants to relax in a lounge."

Day responded to all these objections with logical explanations, but the only response was a hush that fell over the room, punctuated by an occasional "Hummmm" and the rustle of paper.

Cecil Day had had enough. He looked into the sea of doubting eyes, then abruptly stood up.

"Look, gentlemen. Are you going to give me the loan or not?"

Silence. The bankers cast awkward, casual glances around the room. The committee chairman lit a cigar.

"What's it like living in Atlanta?" asked the chairman. "Do children really walk to school barefoot?"

The committee burst into laughter.

Day's face changed from white to pink to blood red. He picked up his briefcase; just before leaving the room, Day grabbed a stack of paper on the desk and threw it down in front of the chairman, knocking the ashes out of his ashtray.

"Gentlemen," he said, "I don't appreciate that remark one bit. When my motels are doing well a year from now, don't bother calling me!" He turned and abruptly left the room, slamming the door behind him.

After six months of searching in the major cities, Day was finally able to convince a banker in his own backyard— in Atlanta—to make a permanent loan.

Cecil didn't have to serve alcohol in order to get the loan, either. In fact, it turned out to be a smart business move for several reasons. As he predicted, insurance rates for his motels without bars were substantially lower than for those with them. Theft of blankets, pillows, towels and other items often taken was down. In addition, vandalism was remarkably low.

The important factor was that Day offered to the family-oriented motorist an alternative in motels. Days Inns were extensions of Day's own value system that made sense.

Faith in God Is Essential

Many business people are God-fearing individuals, but few are ever as bold in their pronouncements about their faith as was Cecil Day. On more than one occasion he told his family and friends, "As I totally depend on Jesus Christ, I continue to grow and feel the assurance of His presence in my life, minute by minute, daily walking with Him, growing in confidence to meet any and all of life's challenges, knowing I am in His will for my life."

Day had accepted Christ as his Savior at the age of eight. However, another dimension of the faith surfaced when he was 27 years old. He and his family attended a religious retreat near Asheville, North Carolina, where they heard a successful businessman speak about reaching maximum potential. "To do this," he said, "a man should subordinate his personal will to the omnipotent will of God, because He loves and knows what is best for His creations. Because He loves us, He wills only the best for us."

At that precise moment, Day understood the concept of lordship. That night, he made a personal commitment to make Christ *Lord* of his life . . . and of his business. Later, as he matured and his business grew, he reinforced his conviction by echoing the words of St. Paul: "I can do all things through Him who strengthens me" (Philippians 4:13).

Cecil Day kept those words in his heart until the day he died.

By 1971, interstate billboards advertised Days Inns motels with the familiar gold sunburst logo promising rooms for "$8 and up." Tourists traveling to and from Walt Disney World were enthusiastic over the concept. The company was already showing profits.

All this began with one man who had a clear vision, an abundance of common sense, a trust in people and a powerful sense of values. All these combined to turn dreams into realities.

Lon L. Day, Sr., a Baptist minister, instilled in his son Cecil a deep appreciation of Judeo-Christian values.

Following Rev. Day's death, Kathleen Burke Day showed Cecil how to apply what his father had taught him.

Cecil Burke Day, Sr.,
at six months of age.

Cecil, age 5, and Lon,
age 10.

Uldine (Deen) Smith (third from left) in her cheerleading days at Mercer University, in Macon, Georgia.

Deen and Cecil meet and fall in love.

Cecil frequently credited the Marine Corps for the discipline it inculcated in him.

One and one-half year-old Burke "guards the fort" while Dad is away.

Cecil graduated from Georgia Tech in June 1958.

Day's first building project was his home. Construction was begun in December 1959 and completed in March 1960.

The Day family in 1962. (Clockwise from top left) Deen, Peyton, Kathie, Burke and Clint.

When Cecil discovered that he had acquired too much real estate, he sold some of his holdings and built this income-producing quadraplex on a remaining piece of property.

Together with builder-friend Tom Fuqua, Day built thousands of apartment units like the one shown here. He later sold them for $14 million.

Behind the modest but efficient check-in counter of the Tybee Days Inn stood Cecil's mother, "Mama Day," and George Spirades. In back of the check-in area was a one-bedroom apartment in which the motel manager lived.

The Forsyth (Georgia) Days Inn was the company's first interstate motel. Unlike the Tybee Island Days Inn, it had a Tasty World restaurant, swimming pool, gas pumps, and a playground. The Forsyth motel was the prototype for future Days Inns, such as the one above.

The first Days Inn opened on Tybee Island, Georgia, in April 1970. The sixty-unit motel had neither a swimming pool, restaurant nor gift shop.

Interior of a typical Days Inns room in the 1970s.

This Tasty World restaurant shares the same roof with a gift shop (background) and a check-in counter.

Gift shops at Days Inns were stocked with the traveling family in mind.

Deen and Cecil in 1972.

(Front, left to right) Kathie, Parke and Peyton. (Rear, left to right) Burke and Clint in 1972.

Cecil congratulates franchise sales director Bob Dollar for his record-breaking sales record in 1973.

Kathie, Art Linkletter, Peyton and Cecil in the new Day Building.

Jo Dollar discusses an agenda with Cecil.

Cecil and Deen listen as columnist/newscaster Paul Harvey addresses employees and guests at a Day Companies Christmas Banquet.

Cecil and Deen stand with Senator Herman Talmadge of Georgia prior to a U. S. Bicentennial Celebration planning session. Cecil served as a state chairman for the "Stay and See Georgia" program, although he admitted that Deen had done "most of the work."

Juanita Gargis (left) and "Mama Day" at a Christmas banquet.

Dave Kenny and his wife, Jo, at a Christmas banquet.

Roger Treadaway and his wife, Ernestine.

Bob Williams and his wife, Gloria.

119

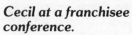
Cecil at a franchisee conference.

"Mama Day" and Roy Burnette chat before a Christmas banquet.

Cecil and associates map out a strategy to erect one thousand Days Inns by 1990.

Tom and Dot Fuqua. Fuqua built almost everything Cecil financed. He and Cecil enjoyed a wonderful friendship and a prosperous business partnership.

121

Under newly-appointed CEO Richard Kessler, Days Inns took on a new look. While the motels grew upwards, the company did not enjoy the growth it had during the early '70s. Shown here is the architect's rendering of one of the first hi-rise Days Inns.

6

When in Trouble, Create

> *"Cecil Day's remarkable ability was demonstrated by the phenomenal success of the business which bears his name—a creative idea which he executed so brilliantly."*
>
> —Bill Bright
> President, Campus
> Crusade for Christ

Paul Harvey, SDC director Rev. Tom Lawler and Cecil before a September Days Club convention. The club was the first ever organized in the lodging industry as an expression of gratitude from Cecil, who gave senior Americans a wooden nickel that was redeemable for a cup of coffee in Tasty World Restaurants. The club neared one million members. SDC members filled fifty percent of Days Inns rooms during the oil embargo.

We'll allow a traveler an opportunity not only to reserve a room at Days Inns but, along with it, a tank of gasoline.

—Cecil B. Day

Sam Collins, an electrical engineer for Westinghouse, was an intelligent man. From the time he blew the top off the S.A.T. scores in high school to the day he graduated magna cum laude from college, he was saluted for his academic prowess.

In business he was destined for success. But Sam Collins fell far short of early expectations.

The reason for his not-so-spectacular climb to success as expected was simple. As long as plans ran smoothly, Sam was able to perform with anyone. Coworkers called him a creative genius because of his innovative ideas. However, once some unexpected problem arose, Sam panicked. Instead of responding with logical solutions, he reacted on impulse, often increasing the severity of the problem.

Sam Collins was an intelligent man, but he surrendered to the demands of problems.

Cecil Day was different. Much different.

In fact, Cecil Day was most creative not when things were flying smoothly or while sunbathing at his Tybee Island beach

125

cottage. He was at his creative best when problems besieged him.

That's just one of the things that separated Cecil Day from the average CEO.

It's easy to be a leader when crowds line the streets in your honor and a strutting drum major leads a parade of marching musicians. Everyone can be a hero when the ticker tape is falling. But what happens when the music stops? To whom do you turn when the crowds that once shouted "Hosanna" now turn their backs and silently walk away? That's the time when a man shows his real character.

Cecil Day was one of those men.

Several times during Cecil's relatively short career, he faced problems that could have spelled disaster for his empire. But part of his genius lay in the fact that he could turn these problems into "opportunities to solve," as he preferred to call them.

In 1976, at 42 years of age, Cecil Day had clearly established himself as an imaginative businessman. He already earned his reputation by using problems as springboards to create four brilliant concepts—"budget luxury," "reserved gasoline," "September Days Club" and his famous "rabbit theory."

Budget Luxury

Most families who vacationed across these United States were limited to the four corners of a tight budget. They could not afford to spend two or three weeks at 50-dollar-a-night hotels. At the same time, they did not want to compromise safety or comfort by staying at cheap, "Skid Row" hotels.

Many independent motel owners were unable to compete with the heavy advertising dollar spent by large chains to attract travelers to their properties. Along the nation's highways, signs that once flashed "NO VACANCY" now read "FOR SALE."

Cecil knew that there was a market out there for the independent motel owner who could provide safety and comfort at a price people could afford. He therefore offered them something he called "budget-luxury motels." These were "Holiday Inns without the frills."

None of his properties had a fancy lobby. "After all," asked Day, "who sleeps in a lobby?" Bellmen were not hired to carry food to individual rooms. Day discovered that customers enjoyed eating in one of the motel's Tasty World restaurants. And no chocolate candy would be put on pillows at night. "Pillows are for weary heads, not Hershey bars," he said.

Each motel room was the same size—12 by 24 feet— with two double beds, a color television set, desk and a bath with a full ceramic shower. The registration desk, a restaurant and a gift shop were all under one roof. Savings on uniform construction costs were passed along to customers.

Reserved Gasoline

The Arab oil embargo of 1973 did more to destroy the motel industry than did anything else in modern times. It threw the nation into a recession and the lodging industry into a full-fledged depression. Families who spent hours waiting in line for gas at local pumps thought twice about driving into strange cities while on vacation, fearing they would be stranded without fuel.

Days Inns were not immune to the aftershock of the embargo. Occupancy had dropped to a dismal 45 percent nationwide. While this figure may have been acceptable to higher priced, older hotels built during periods of lower construction costs and interest rates, it was unacceptable for Days Inns that depended on 60 percent occupancy just to pay the bills.

Day's creative juices, combined with his eerie sense of

prophecy, led him to include with each motel built along the interstates a gasoline pump. This was something unheard of in the motel trade; nonetheless, it proved to be the perfect answer to the problem.

"We'll allow a traveler an opportunity not only to reserve a room at Days Inns but, along with it, a tank of gasoline," said Cecil. That guaranteed a family rest for the night, plus enough fuel to drive for the better part of the day to the Days Inns at their next stop.

The news media got word of the innovative concept. Commentators, such as the popular Paul Harvey, mentioned this plan on national broadcasts. Also, all three television networks applauded the plan.

Even the once-caustic skeptics didn't laugh at this idea. Everyone saw the wisdom in it.

The idea was not without its problems, however. Not only was gasoline scarce and expensive, but also the Department of Energy had drafted a plan whereby fuel would be allocated on a percentage of the retailer's past year's sales. Gasoline wholesalers were reluctant to sell fuel to someone not officially in the gas sales business.

Cecil appointed Roger Treadaway to head a newly created division: "Gasoline Department."

"We had to beg and borrow gasoline from almost anyone having it," Treadaway remembers. Major wholesalers wanted purchasers to produce a one million dollar line of credit from banks before they'd even consider selling gasoline to an applicant.

The Government allocated each state with a fixed amount of gasoline and forced Cecil and Treadaway to spend a tremendous amount of time requesting more allotments from the Department of Energy.

"Cecil was uniquely situated in this regard," says Treadaway. "Since he owned the motels we service, dried up gas pumps in heavily traveled areas—such as Orlando—benefited from the reserves we were allowed in Atlanta. We paid independent truckers to haul gas where it was most needed."

The demand surpassed all expectations. As quickly as it was pumped from the truck into 10,000-gallon underground storage tanks, the gas was sold. Although gasoline was offered to customers at a discount (Day could have charged premium rates but didn't), total profits surpassed those at the restaurants and gift shops combined.

The gasoline turned a healthy profit for Cecil. More importantly, it turned what could have been a death blow to his business into a source that filled his rooms to nearly full occupancy.

There were no "FOR SALE" signs on Days Inns properties that year.

September Days Club

"Cecil, you've got to upgrade your image," laughed a New York public relations man when he saw the people leaving one of the Atlanta motels. "You've got nothing but a bunch of old folks here. They're burdens. They're not going to be around much longer. You've got to appeal to young people. That's your future."

That counsel may have been accepted by the less imaginative motel owner. Others may have regarded older clientele as "burdens," but not Cecil Day. Once again, he took what others deemed to be a problem and created from it a winning combination.

Perhaps that's why Cecil never sought the advice of New York P.R. men, but looked within his own ranks for solutions to problems. Usually that's where the best answers came from.

Day and his staff agreed that senior citizens were virtually an untapped market in the motel business. They wondered why. After all, seniors rarely stole items; they were neater on the average than their younger counterparts; they were more conscientious about the way they left rooms; they were loyal to the company in that they returned year after year on vacations; and even though they had plenty of cash, they were budget-minded.

Other businessmen throughout the nation may have agreed with the New York P.R. man and looked upon the elderly as necessary evils who had to be endured. Cecil realized that this untapped market of America's seniors would be a tremendous source of income.

He made his first move in the fall of '75 when he gave "wooden nickels" to senior citizens—50 years and older—redeemable for a cup of coffee at Tasty World restaurants. Recipients were also asked to fill out forms, with their names and addresses, and drop them into a designated container on the registration desk.

A few thousand people filled out these forms during the first month. Cecil personally signed "thank you" notes to each person.

The promotion caught on. In three months, about 22,000 names were added to the computer mailing list. The "wooden nickel" became popular. By the fall of '76, Cecil's personal letters expanded to a 36-page four-color quarterly magazine he entitled *September Days*.

Within a few months, the mailing list neared a half million names. That astonished even the optimistic Cecil Day. The group identified as a "problem" by others had developed into a supportive clientele through the insights of Cecil Day.

Rev. Tam Lawler was appointed to the full-time position as September Days Club Executive Director. Under his leadership the club hosted its first national convention in April 1976. Response to the ad placed in *September Days* was no less than overwhelming. Over 1,400 people from throughout the United States gathered in Atlanta to meet and share experiences. The only thing they had in common was a stay at one of the nation's Days Inns properties.

Less than one year later, a separate "Convention and Tour" department branched out of the September Days Club. It enrolled even more members. Many of them shared trips to Jamaica and other vacation spots. Future conventions featured nationally known speakers, including Bob Hope, Art Linkletter, Paul Harvey and Kirby ("Sky King") Grant.

Some of Day's new managers encouraged him to sell ads in his magazine to offset some of its enormous overhead. The ads offered discounted prescriptions or group insurance.

"I don't want to exploit these people," said Cecil. "They have been very good to the chain. These senior Americans have stayed with us during the embargo. They helped us keep our jobs. I want them treated not as commercial commodities but as our special guests."

The continued support of senior citizens proved again that Cecil Day was right. To this day, senior citizens remain loyal to Days Inns. They occupy a major portion of each motel. And the current administration sees firsthand the fruits of Cecil Day's ability to create profits out of problems.

The Rabbit Theory

During the money-lean years of the Arab oil embargo, Cecil constantly had to create ways of keeping apprehensive bankers calm. When the economic climate raised the anxiety levels of these guardians of financial institutions, they often called for their money, and they wanted it *now!* Cecil, therefore, had to create for each banker and vendor unique, innovative ways of repayment.

Cecil reached into his grab bag of creative ideas and developed something still spoken of today in the business community. Cecil called it his "rabbit theory."

It was not something that he learned from listening to sophisticated lectures on finance or from any other business "guru." Instead, he recalled a scene from a cowboy movie he saw as a youngster.

The leading man in the movie had been out hunting rabbits for the better part of an afternoon. The hunter had a splendid day with his rifle. One hour before sunset, he had a bag filled to overflowing with rabbits. The cowboy grunted as he slung over his horse's back and headed for home.

Suddenly, his horse acted strangely. Its gait became erratic. The cowboy looked over his shoulder. A pack of wolves was in hot pursuit of the cowboy and his horse.

Beads of sweat quickly surfaced on the cowboy's brow. He thrust his spurs into the sides of the horse. The horse reared into the air, then galloped toward safety at the cowboy's prairie home.

The horse ran as fast as his legs would carry him and his rider, yet the pack of wolves quickly gained ground. Soon, they nipped at the horse's tail.

The cowboy's face lit up. "Maybe," he said to himself, in a John Wayne-type drawl, "they're after these dad-burned rabbits."

As the horse continued rushing toward home, still miles away, the cowboy reached into his rabbit bag, pulled one out and tossed it high into the air behind him. The wolves suddenly stopped and devoured the rabbit. The cowboy let out a sigh of relief, then slowed his horse to a more relaxing trot.

His confidence was short-lived, however. Within a few minutes, the wolves once again pursued him. This time, they seemed even hungrier than before.

Again, the cowboy kicked his horse into high gear, and threw out another rabbit . . . then another . . . one at a time. Each time a rabbit hit the ground, the wolf pack stopped for as long as it took to eat it.

Finally, the cowboy saw his house off in the distance. Looking over his shoulder once more, he saw the wolves still pursuing him. He reached into his rabbit bag and fumbled through it. Only one rabbit remained.

"Oh-oh. This rabbit is supposed to be tonight's stew," he said, "and I gotta feed the little lady at home."

The wolves were now nipping at the horse's hoofs.

"The heck with supper!" he yelled to the highest heavens, as he tossed the last rabbit to the pack. The wolves stopped long enough to allow the cowboy and his horse to make it safely behind the fence surrounding his home.

The cowboy dismounted, then pulled his rifle and empty rabbit sack off the horse. With the look of a defeated warrior, he walked into the house.

His wife stood beside a hearth where a porridge pot hung above a blazing fire.

"I don't see any rabbits in your bag," she chided.

"I know," sighed her husband. "The blasted wolves got 'em."

"But what are we going to eat?" she lamented. "We're going to starve."

"No, we're not," shot back the cowboy. "I *still* have my horse and rifle. Tomorrow I can go hunting again."

Cecil Day compared bankers to that pack of wolves. When economic conditions were uncertain—such as during the Arab oil embargo—some bankers were tempted to demand that a loan be called and immediately paid in full. Before the banker could make the demand, Cecil offered to pay enough to keep him happy for a while. In the meantime, Cecil gained enough time to work with his employees in creating new ideas that would eventually earn enough profits to repay the loan—ahead of schedule if at all possible.

Many of Cecil's successful ideas came from the most unexpected sources—problems. At least, they came from what others *thought* were problems.

Had Sam Collins known Cecil Day, he just might have been the success his friends had predicted.

The Day family participates in Kathie's wedding, held in Dunwoody Baptist Church. Not even cancer kept Cecil from escorting his daughter down the aisle. It was the last time Cecil was to walk without assistance. (Left to right) Parke, Clint, Deen, Kathie, Cecil, Peyton and Burke.

7

Gain Family Support

Yes, Cecil Day was a successful role model for young businessmen today. And yes, he was a committed Christian and faithful steward.

However, another dimension of his life that needs to be shared was his love and respect for his wife, Deen, and for his family. They brought "balance" to his life. Deen was his inspiration, his prayer partner, his business confidante and his best friend. He was totally devoted to her and the family.

This was my greatest impression of Cecil Day.

—JoAnn F. Dollar
Former Executive
Assistant to Cecil B. Day

Cecil and Deen at the 1975 Day Companies Christmas banquet, which was always attended by the employees' children and relatives. Nobody doubted that Deen was Cecil's best friend and closest confidant.

*You can't fire God or your family. You might lose every-
thing you own because of one bad decision, but God and
family will be there, regardless.*

—Cecil B. Day

Herman W. Lay, founder of Frito-Lay, once said, "A
man makes his success by the decisions that he
himself makes, and by when he makes them." To
this Cecil Day would have added, "Unless a man is an island
filled with *himself,* he is wise to gain the support of others,
expecially his family."

Cecil Day practiced what he preached. Seldom did he
step into a new endeavor without making us family members
aware of his ideals, goals and game plan. He didn't seek
our *permission* as much as he did our *perspectives*. He fully
realized that whatever affected him would leave a profound
impact on us as well.

There was the time one evening at home just after dinner.
Nearly everything was normal that night. Seated around the
oval dining table in their usual chairs were Kathie, age 13;
Clint, 10; Peyton, 8; and Parke, 5. I always sat next to my
father at mealtime. Mom sat at the far end of the table.
At the age of 15, I was just beginning to understand my
role as eldest son.

As I said, *nearly* everything was normal. Only one thing

was noticeably different. Dad, who was sitting in his chair at the head of the table, was uncharacteristically dressed for the meal. He was wearing a coat and tie, rather than his usual attire—pajamas. More than once throughout the course of the meal, we children cast suspicious glances at him as if something wasn't quite right.

"As soon as you're finished eating," Cecil ordered, with an unusual tone of seriousness in his voice, "I would like everybody to meet with me in the family room." He rose from his chair and left the room.

The rest of us quickly ate what was left on our plates—a standing order at home. We then gathered together in the family room. My father stood beside an easel, which held a large paper drawing pad. Next to him stood Mom.

Selling the Family

Once everyone got comfortable, 36-year-old Cecil Day began to speak not as a father to his family, but as though he were addressing his board of directors.

"I have an idea," he began, as he cleared his throat, "and I believe it will work."

A pause filled the room. Peyton and Parke covered their mouths in an attempt to smother their giggles at the business-like demeanor directed at them.

"As you know, we have two motel properties—the one on Tybee Island and the other on Interstate 75 near Forsyth."

He paused again. One raised eyebrow quickly silenced my two giggling brothers.

"These motels are doing well, and I believe we can build a thousand of them by 1990. Maybe even by 1980," he added.

We suspected that our father was on the brink of something special. His salesman's voice was in high gear.

For the next hour, Cecil Day walked through his plan to expand Days Inns. He flipped over large pages from the easel and spoke with a polished prose normally reserved for bankers and other people of gargantuan influence. His speaking style was deliberate and formal, yet his eyes sparkled with the enthusiasm of a tent-meeting evangelist.

His eyebrows rose up and down when punctuating parts of his speech or pressing a point such as his deep-rooted belief that Days Inns could become the "McDonald's of the lodging industry."

We listened intently, interrupting only if he used a word or phrase one of us didn't understand. Once he explained it to our satisfaction, he continued.

At the conclusion of his dissertation, he heaved a long sigh, then said, "To do this, I need your support. Can I count on it?"

"Yes!" I said, as unelected spokesman for the group. By now I was caught up in his enthusiasm.

"Good," said Cecil. Now, we'll vote on it.

We looked at each other. Clinton shrugged his shoulders. Kathie simply raised her eyebrows. But none of the others was smiling. I must admit, the whole idea was overwhelming.

"All those in favor, please raise your hand."

Five hands, including Cecil's, shot up in the air. My mother's remained by her side, as did Clint's.

Cecil's face dimmed. His sales pitch wasn't as convincing as he had hoped.

"Okay, let's discuss this further," he said, with a gentle, matter-of-fact tone in his voice.

The room fell silent again.

Breaking the stillness, our mother spoke first.

"I think you children need to know more about the cost of this in terms of our family life." Her voice was hushed, yet filled with maternal caution.

"Your mother's right," Cecil explained. "I won't be home as much as usual. I'll be traveling a great deal. Each of you will have to be even more responsible for yourselves." Again he paused, staring at a blank wall. He appeared hesitant to continue, but he did. "I feel that God is calling me to do this. But I confess that I don't want to do this alone. I need your support."

"It's also going to be a greater burden on me," added Mom.

Cecil expected her to continue, but his wife said no more.

"Clint," Cecil probed, "what are your thoughts?"

"Well, sort of like Mom said," answered the ten-year-old, "I'd like having you around more."

"I can appreciate that," Cecil replied, smiling, "just as I'd rather be here with you. But there's a price, son, on achieving great things. Opportunities like this don't just happen. You've got to *make* them happen."

"Burke," Cecil asked, "what do you think?"

Without the slightest hesitation I offered my opinion. "If you feel led by God to do it, I encourage you to do it."

"Kathie?"

"I trust your judgment, Daddy. If anyone can do it, you can."

"Peyton?"

"How can you build a thousand motels by yourself?" he asked with a serious tone that imitated Dad.

"I can't do it alone," Cecil ansered. "That's one reason why I need everyone's support here at home."

"Parke?"

"Can they all have swimming pools?" asked his youngest.

Smiling, Cecil answered, "Maybe."

Cecil Day put it to the vote again. This time he gained the unanimous support he sought. Triumphantly, he smiled. But before dismissing everyone for the night, he asked us all to kneel with him in prayer before launching into his new endeavor.

A Most Practical Dimension

The family support my father sought from us was far from a condescending gesture. As with so many of his choices, he saw a practical side to this approach.

Support of his family provided Cecil with something he would never have gained from a Dale Carnegie course, from professionals working in his offices, or from the most sophisticated computer. In fact, many of his more successful ideas resulted from his listening to words that came from the proverbial "babe's mouth."

Consider the innocent question raised by Parke.

The first Days Inns built on Tybee Island was successful by anyone's standards. Yet it lacked any child's most hoped-for amenity away from home—a swimming pool.

Parke, Peyton and Clint—my three younger brothers—often complained, "Every other motel has a swimming pool, and their managers keep chasing us away if we use them. Why doesn't Days Inns have one?"

"You've got the biggest pool in the world just a block away—the beach," Cecil shot back, chuckling.

But my brothers never let up. Almost daily, they lamented the fact that if Days Inns had a pool, they could use it. Still, Dad wouldn't budge, claiming, "It's too expensive. Besides, the occupancy is almost 100 percent. Why fix something that's not broken?"

Two years later, occupancy at the Tybee Days Inns showed a steady decline. Unbeknownst to my brothers was the fact that the motel's manager also strongly suggested a pool be added so he could remain competitive with other inns on the island.

The following June, Cecil drove his family down to Tybee for yet another summer vacation. This time, however, he didn't stop at his small beach cottage.

"Dad," Clinton yelled from the station wagon's back seat. "You just passed the cottage."

"Oh," Cecil replied, faking a mistake.

He drove four blocks farther, then turned into the parking lot of the Days Inns.

"Oh, boy!" shouted Peyton.

"Dad, you're the greatest," said young Parke.

The three youngest sons leaped out of the car and raced to the edge of a newly installed swimming pool.

"Isn't Dad great?" Peyton remarked as Cecil discussed the rising rate of occupancy with the manager. "He built this pool just for us."

This coincidental gift elevated Cecil even more in his children's eyes. It made us feel more a part of his effort. Yet there were more serious sides to my father's rationale of gaining family support.

A Source of Ideas

The Day family dinner table often proved itself a database of ideas or suggestions brought in by us children or our mother. Sometimes the source of this input was someone who at school, at a football game or at a civic function made a simple remark to one of us.

Late one afternoon, for instance, I came home from school and echoed a friend's complaint that the Tybee Island Days Inns wasn't fun because it had no playground. Cecil saw to it that the next motel and successive ones did. When the same young friend voiced his parents' complaint that not all Days Inns had the same room rates, Cecil made certain that room rates for each motel were listed in Days Inns' national directory, so that each family could select a motel in terms of both location and price.

Volunteer Help

On lengthy, interstate trips with his family, it wasn't an uncommon sight seeing Cecil Day's family eating at a Tasty World restaurant. While we were there, if Cecil saw a customer lifting an empty coffee cup to a busy waitress, he prompted one of us to get a fresh pot and fill the cup.

If the restaurant had a desperate shortage of help, Cecil and us sons "volunteered" to clean tables and wash dishes. Mom sometimes filled in as hostess, and Kathie worked as cashier. As we drove away from the restaurant, Dad remarked, *"We"*—that was his favorite pronoun—"make a good team. Thanks for your help."

Cecil Day always listened with interest to what his family had to suggest. This isn't to imply that he always accepted our ideas. Most of the time, in fact, he didn't. On rare occasions, a remark even drew his rebuke.

The Banquet "Sermon"

During a company Christmas party one year, the guest speaker, hoping, perhaps, to please Cecil, delivered a 60-minute religious talk that sounded very much like a Sunday morning sermon. I sat with my brothers and sister near the head table. We couldn't help but notice that many of the people who filled the ballroom yawned a great deal. Some barely kept their heads up. Many constantly checked their watches, while others strained to pay attention.

Later that evening, at home, my father asked me what I thought of the program.

"Dad, I don't think it's fair what you did tonight," I replied.

The glow left my father's face.

"What do you mean?" he asked, clearing his throat and furrowing a brow.

"Well," I said, looking to the ceiling for just the right

words, "not everybody working with you shares the same faith. They all more or less *have* to attend the Christmas party and listen to what's said from the podium. Tonight, a lot of people were also bored." After a silent pause I added, "If it were me, I'd feel trapped into listening."

Anticipating his reply, I ducked my head into my shoulders like a turtle withdrawing into its shell.

"No one *has* to come to my party," he blurted. "It's my party, and I pay for it. Whoever pays the piper can pick the song he wishes to hear."

I offered no rebuttal. An awkward silence told me there was nothing more to say. I turned to leave the room, seriously wondering whether or not I should have even answered his question.

"Oh . . . Burke. . . ." The voice was soft, but I had no trouble hearing it. "Thanks a lot for being honest with me."

I looked back. A gentle smile crossed his face.

A Source of Comfort

Whether or not Cecil Day realized it, by soliciting his family's input, by listening to our remarks, answering our questions and encouraging us to raise other questions, he was planting seeds of corporate concern in our hearts. If motel occupancy fell, we did whatever we could to encourage him when he came home with a whipped puppy dog look on his face.

Mom was the one who could best ascertain Dad's needs as soon as he walked into the house. There was something about the way he closed the door that cued her either to give him time alone or to pamper him by washing his back as he bathed in a hot tub.

We children had our own way of helping our father to relax.

Rather than lament about the worst part of our day, we

told our father about the positives we experienced. I'll admit I inherited my father's impulse for cutting classes. Therefore, I stressed what I learned in the geometry class I attended rather than confess to skipping English class. Kathie spoke of her cheerleading in upcoming football games. Clint, Peyton and Parke spoke of their football heroics on the practice field that day. Just as Cecil Day was an encouraging father, his zeal for accentuating the positive boomeranged back to him when he needed an uplift.

"I picture this home as a port," Cecil often said at the dinner table, "and me as a battle-scarred boat about to sink. But after one brief stop here, I feel like a mended, rearmed battleship ready to go back out and face whatever's ahead of me."

The Voice of the Consumer

There was another offer that came freely from family members, one that acted as a sounding board for the consumer.

Cecil Day realized that consumer honesty came easier from family members than from any other source. The consumers themselves may not have known what they wanted, but they sure knew what they didn't like. As for his employees, few, if any, had an opportunity to complain to a pajama-clad CEO, no matter how straightforward they might want to be. Moreover, just about everyone carried a hidden desire to say only what he or she thought the employer *wanted* to hear.

On the other hand, all of us realized that the dinner table was a sanctuary where we could confess honest concerns, without fear of expulsion. As Cecil often voiced it, "You can't fire God or your family. You might lose everything you own because of one bad decision, but God and family will be there, regardless."

Some psychologists insist that a business executive

should be willing to close the office door at five o'clock and leave all his problems in the office before coming home. Cecil Day didn't buy that philosophy. Instead, he brought home and openly talked with his wife and children about the joys and disappointments of his working day. He made us feel almost like joint-founders.

The dining room table became an informal conference table at which he discussed even his conversations earlier that day with employees or business associates. He spoke about a remark made by some prophet of doom. He spoke candidly about his frustrations at not knowing the best course of action to take in a given situation. I guess one of the greatest honors he ever paid us children was when he asked any one of us what we would have done in a similar situation.

These were not gossip sessions. Far from it. Instead, they were golden opportunities for this CEO to educate his family, make each of us feel important and, perhaps most importantly, make us a working part of his "extended team," which he had left back at the office that afternoon.

All of us children eventually worked in his business at some point in our lives. But there were no special guarantees or privileges. To the contrary, when any one of us children worked for him, it was usually under the direction of another employee. Our bosses were given the instruction by our own father that if we didn't work out, they should fire us. And he would support the decision.

This strategy provided for Cecil a priceless insurance policy. By blending the input of his own family with those responsible for the day by day operations of his business, he was molding a kinship that would pay rich dividends for years to come. Neither his family nor his employees would be strangers to one another, but personalities with whom each of us could easily identify.

Cecil Day realized that if he were to die unexpectedly, his legacy would have a much better chance of surviving him if this kinship was tightly knitted through mutual respect.

In all honesty, his family and close associates never gave this much thought. After all, this young, vibrant, energetic leader was a picture of health. Plans for creating a legacy were normally left to senior citizens who had more reason and more time to make such plans.

At age 43, when our father, suffering from terminal cancer, was rushed from his home to the hospital, every one of us realized the wisdom behind his thinking.

8

Fight the Giants

Cecil Day was a kind and gentle warrior.

—Hal Northrop,
President and CEO,
Callaway Gardens

The first of the Days Inns was built on Tybee Island, Georgia, in spite of numerous protests that Cecil should not enter the motel business. It contained 60 rooms and had neither a restaurant nor a swimming pool. When this motel opened, every room was filled with guests who paid $8.00 a night.

I am grateful for pressure; without pressure, water couldn't come out of a showerhead.

—Cecil B. Day

The Bible tells a familiar story of a small shepherd boy who sat one afternoon on a large rock, stretching a wet leather string. When it was just about the right size, he placed it on the rock and let it dry in the hot sun. As soon as it was dry enough, he strung it through a hole in his brown sling and tied it securely, repairing the slingshot he used each day to protect his sheep from hungry wolves.

Suddenly, a friend ran toward him with a look of sheer terror on his face. "David," gasped his friend, "the Philistines have this powerful giant!"

"So?" asked David as he inspected his newly repaired sling.

"He's challenged to fight any one of our people. If he wins, then Israel will become the servants of the Philistines."

"Oh?" replied David. "And what's his name?"

"They call him 'Goliath,'" the friend continued, still gasping for air. "And there's no one around who is willing to fight him."

David stopped repairing his sling and looked his friend squarely in the eye. "Why haven't they asked me?"

David's friend almost burst out laughing. How could a boy in his teens expect to fight and win against a giant such as Goliath?

But the friend realized David was serious. Since no one else from Israel volunteered to go into battle, David prepared to fight Goliath to the death.

Two days later, David stood in the shadow of Goliath. The giant, fully armored, looked down at his teenage foe and laughed out loud. "Is this what you sent against me?" he asked.

David reached into a small bag, took out a stone, placed it into his sling and let it fly. The stone struck Goliath between the eyes. The giant fell with a mighty *"THUD!"* Israel remained a free nation, because one overmatched, brave soul dared to fight the giant.

It is not stretching the point to say that every person who hopes to win in the business world also must fight some powerful giants. Cecil Day was not immune to this fact.

The giants Cecil faced were not much different from those whom others in business must face. Cecil's giants were: banks, friends, stress, worry and pride.

The giants may be familiar to us. Cecil's way of fighting them was unique.

To reach his dreams, Cecil Day had to deal with each of these giants. Although he didn't have to kill them as did David, he had to conquer them sufficiently to use them to his advantage.

Banks

The first giant was the banking industry.

More often than any other source, this group of historically conservative investors kept arguing with Day that his ideas wouldn't work—despite the fact that Cecil already had two motels operating at a profit.

Day built and opened the Forsyth motel three months

after the Tybee Island property. In Forsyth, Day proved that his concept could work even on a larger scale. The Forsyth project, for example, had 120 rooms—twice the number at Tybee. In addition, the Forsyth motel included a Tasty World restaurant and a gift shop. About 20 strides away was a roofed gasoline island with self-service pumps.

Each room at the Forsyth motel followed the "budget-luxury" pattern at Tybee. In addition, it had a playground for children and a swimming pool. It was a far cry from any "mom and pop" operation that other banks were willing to finance.

Hence, Cecil, who now planned to build 14 more units like the Forsyth motel, thought he should have no problem obtaining necessary financing. Cecil was wrong.

Cecil's track record notwithstanding, banker after banker insisted that a motel would flop within a year unless the owner was willing to sell alcoholic beverages in its restaurants. But Cecil never gave in. Backed by logic and a burning belief that serving alcohol would violate his conscience as a Christian businessman, he eventually convinced enough bankers that his plan would work. He showed, for instance, how the absence of alcohol would result in less damage to property, less stolen items such as sheets and towels, and lower insurance rates. In short, he would be able to operate at a less fixed-cost basis than would others in the industry. The banks listened, agreed and eventually made the loans.

Another tactic Cecil used to gain the confidence of bankers was during those times he owed a bank money and could not repay all of the loan. Instead of avoiding them, he boldly walked into the bank, saw the banker in person, admitted his problem and worked things out so that the bank would eventually be paid on a schedule that Cecil could handle. Bankers thought even more of him once he repaid them.

Later, when money became exceptionally tight, Cecil had gained so much confidence within the banking industry that he was still able to borrow money. Many other motel owners, with their fancy lounges, were politely turned away empty-handed.

Fighting his giant of banks sometimes called for unorthodox tactics. One particularly stubborn banker, for example, was reluctant to loan money for constructing motels. Cecil knew, however, that this particular banker often bragged about his air-conditioned office, automobile and home. "Air-conditioning did for the South what furnaces did for the North," he often told Cecil.

During one exceptionally hot summer day in 1972, Cecil arranged to meet with this banker to discuss the possibility of a much-needed loan. Cost overruns on a particular site made a loan an absolute necessity if the motel was to be constructed.

Instead of meeting him for lunch, Cecil suggested that the banker ride with him to the construction site. The banker agreed.

That morning, Cecil asked his oldest son if he could borrow the teen's car—a stripped-down, 1971 Pinto, with no radio, no cigarette lighter and no air conditioning.

The temperature was in the upper 90s. The humidity seemed just as high when Cecil picked up the banker in the Pinto. During their hour-long tour of the site, the banker gave one excuse after another as to why he wasn't able to honor the loan request.

Sweat poured from the banker's face. He frequently mopped his forehead with a handkerchief. "Let's get back to my office. This heat is killing me," he pleaded.

Cecil also felt uncomfortable, but he kept talking about the loan, stressing its importance for the completion of the property they just visited. The banker refused to budge, but Cecil continued to plead, just as the heat continued to build.

"Okay! Okay!" shouted the banker. "You can have your loan. But—just get me back to the bank!"

Cecil did. Somehow the heat didn't bother him anymore.

Friends

Many well-intentioned friends didn't want to see Day venture out farther than they thought he should. Although he listened with interest to what his friends advised, Cecil knew he could win with his philosophy.

Those who worked closely with Cecil during his apartment-building and fast-food-operating days were often the biggest giants he had to face. That became particularly apparent during one meeting with business partners.

Prior to that meeting, Cecil, for some unexplained reason, got into his car alone. He had no specific destination; he just drove. All day he drove northward on the interstates until he became too tired, pulled off the expressway and checked into a Howard Johnson's motel somewhere in Virginia.

He carried only two items into his room—a Bic pen and a legal-sized notepad. He didn't even bring a change of clothes or toiletries.

He lay on the bed and slept for two hours. Suddenly he woke, jumped out of bed and sat at the tiny desk in the room. He picked up his pen and wrote on the legal pad for 14 straight hours—taking time not even for meal breaks.

He placed the last period on the last sheet of paper, returned to bed and slept soundly until the next morning.

When he returned to Atlanta, he called four of his longtime business associates—his brother, Lon; Bill Hitson, who was part of Day Realty Associates; Tom Fuqua, his home and apartment building partner; and Charlie Wild, his restaurant operating partner. Cecil also invited to the meeting Dave Kenney, another restaurant operating partner, with the understanding that he would have no voting power, along with Richard Kessler, a recent Georgia Tech graduate who was to take notes of the meeting.

Day explained to the assembled group the plan he had outlined on his legal pad the night before. He then opened the floor for discussion.

"The motel business?" asked one, scratching his head. "Why in the world should we go into the motel business?"

"Yeah," agreed another. "We've just sold some apartments that proved to be fantastic for us."

"I don't know, Cecil," said Lon with a big brother tone to his voice. "It may not be the thing to do."

"I agree," said Tom. "It's too risky."

Day listened patiently to the pros and cons each man offered. Then he called for a vote.

The vote was split. Hitson and Wild voted "Yes"; the other two said, "No." It was noon, so Cecil suspended the meeting for lunch.

Cecil called for another vote following lunch. The results were the same. So Cecil broke the tie with his "Yes" vote. Then he gave each voting man a unique opportunity. Each could buy ten percent of the new company for only 100 dollars. No one passed by that opportunity.

Each of Day's friends voted a heartfelt concern, but had Cecil not voted his conviction, Days Inns would have been only a fleeting dream.

Stress

Usually, stress is that powerful force that drains or deforms things. It can take a disastrous toll on a person's mental and physical well-being. Cecil knew it could create pressure, yet to him pressure was not always bad; it could also work for good.

"Without pressure," he once said, "water couldn't come out of a showerhead. I'm grateful for pressure; it keeps toilets flushing."

One kind of stress did bother Cecil—the thought of not

living up to a commitment. Any hint of not repaying a loan to a bank or any other investor was abominable.

Therefore, Day had to subdue this giant before it got to a point where he lost control. As he did with banks, he arranged to pay off his debts—with higher interest, if necessary—over a longer period of time.

Worry

Cecil Day had every reason to worry and be fearful during the Arab oil embargo of 1973. He had made pledges to churches, banks, individuals, and employees who looked to him for paychecks. Yet Cecil faced this crisis with an unusual calm. While he watched many friends fail in business, even read of others committing suicide because they were unwilling to face an uncertain future, Cecil refused to worry about tomorrow.

"Something I'll never understand," he told his sons, "is why some people waste an hour of my time telling me how there was nothing they could do to solve their problems. They claim they have no answers. But as soon as they leave my office, they think nothing of walking to a corner drugstore and buying a thick book of crossword *puzzles*.

"These people cheat themselves out of a wonderful opportunity—the chance to discover the real-life, problem-solving genius that lies within them. They'd rather worry about their problems.

"Worry, like a bunch of buzzards, circles its victim who is too concerned about things over which he has no control. I refuse to worry about such things. Those I turn over to God. The things that are placed in my control, I work hard at fixing, mending or maintaining."

Pride

This was the one giant Cecil Day had to fight more than

any other. Especially during his first years of marriage, his pride was as large as Goliath's shadow. In business as well as at home, Cecil insisted that things go *his* way or *no* way at all.

The first signs of conquering that giant came at a family retreat to Ridgecrest, North Carolina, in 1961, when he subordinated his will to that of his Maker. Over the years that attitude matured, and Cecil was able to master his pride.

Cecil Day never claimed to be the smartest guy in the world, but he never classified himself as the dumbest, either. So in business, he focused on what he considered his God-given gifts of creativity and organizational structuring.

Frankly, after his long record of successes, Cecil could have had an inflated ego that would certainly have stifled the progress of his business. An overstuffed ego, for instance, invites the chief executive officer to hire only "yes people" who feed his concept of self-worth.

To guard against this giant overtaking him, Cecil did just the opposite. He kept his sights on reaching objectives and hired better trained experts to run the day-by-day activities. He surrounded himself with people whom he considered more intelligent in certain areas of expertise. It may not have been the best for his ego, but it sure paid dividends in business.

* * *

The giants that Cecil Day faced were always around the corner, just as they are for everyone who ventures into the cold, cruel world of business. Cecil never avoided them. Instead, he met them head-on, mastered them, and became his own giant.

But Cecil Day was different from Goliath.

He knew how to bow his head.

9

Keep Up the Teamwork

If more people conducted their business as did Cecil Day, we would have a sounder, more efficient, trustworthy environment in which to conduct our business.

—Curtis Cheshire,
Trust Company Bank,
Group V.P. (Retired) Atlanta

Day Companies Christmas banquets were always well attended. The first company parties were held in the Days' home. As the Day Companies grew, Deen requested that Cecil move the evergrowing parties to ballrooms or that he enlarge the house. Cecil swiftly decided to host the Christmas parties in large ballrooms, as shown.

I'll always be grateful to Cecil Day and the opportunity he gave me. I've tried emulating his conduct in my business—and it works.

—Roy Burnette

It was a time for celebration. Employee spirits ran high at the nationwide reception of the Days Inns concept in 1973. The hoopla grew even louder when the employees learned that Days Inns was now the fastest growing chain in the world.

The childhood lesson Cecil learned while flying a kite was paying off. By following the "tug" that pulled at his heart and directed him, his empire had grown from one "no-name motel on a no-name island" to a total of 188 open or under construction in only 29 months.

The new eight-story Day Building was a prestigious move to more luxurious quarters, according to most of the enthusiastic employees. To Cecil it was merely a necessary shell of a building that he needed to accommodate his fast-growing companies.

Day Realty branched into new divisions. Real estate companies now bore Day's name in Orlando, Dallas, Atlanta, Albany, Savannah, Charlotte and Richmond.

Days Lodges

In 1971, Cecil expanded his hospitality business by creating a new company—Days Lodges.

Days Lodges were as large as the one-bedroom apartments Cecil had built when he was primarily in the apartment building business. They had a living room equipped with a dining table, sofa-bed, coffee and end tables. The full-sized kitchen was completely furnished with a refrigerator, a sink with a disposal, a dishwasher and cabinet space that would please any homemaker. Even plates, knives and forks were included. A large bedroom came furnished with two double beds and a vanity. A sliding glass door opened to a small outside patio. All this rented for only $12.88 a night—another example of Day's "budget-luxury" concept.

Both short-term construction loans and long-term notes were not that much of a problem for future franchisees. The Day Mortgage Company was paid a percentage—usually one or two points—on loans it secured for people building Days Inns.

Soon the corporate organizational chart looked like a street map of New York City. Different companies bearing Day's name branched out in all directions.

Not only did these new companies handle everyday operational problems better than the Atlanta office, they added to company morale. That was important to Cecil.

Day knew that a young, rapidly growing and successful company such as Days Inns attracted employees who reflected the entrepreneur spirit in himself. These personalities with strong drives and steel-trap minds were valuable to the company. At the same time, Cecil knew they could be destructive if not properly motivated. "The competitive spirit of a prizefighter is admirable," he once said, "as long as he abides by the rules of boxing."

Applauding Employees

Day operated his business on an "Indian/Chief" concept. "Indians" stayed at the main village (offices) and made certain that everything ran smoothly. Meanwhile, Day—the "Chief"—was out hunting buffalo (money or motel sites).

Day wasn't afraid to surround himself with intelligent, innovative employees. In fact, he sought them out. He realized that a horizontal organization worked better than a vertical structure in his business.

Day learned the benefits of that concept years earlier from Scott Hudgens. Scott gave an employee room to grow by not setting down too many rules and regulations. As a result, employees saw quicker promotions and salary increases than do many people in a lifetime.

Instead of taking the bows himself, Day adopted the approach of his father and became a motivator, applauding his employees for work well done.

Day waved banners equally for those who couldn't fare as well as other employees. He realized that everyone on the team was important to the success of his operation. And he wanted everyone to know his feelings about that.

One employee, for example, casually mentioned to Cecil that a suggestion box should be placed in the building. Day liked the idea so much that he had one installed near the corporation lunchroom. But it didn't stop here. Day read many suggestions placed in that box and often used an employee's idea, giving full credit to the one who suggested it.

Although the suggestions were valued, the employees themselves were of even more concern to Cecil. On several occasions he was approached by stock market brokerages who proposed making the company "public." Day was firm in his response. "If anyone is to get Days Inns stock," he told them, "it will be an employee."

Building on Faith

Having established himself as a Christian businessman in the marketplace, Cecil attracted others who shared not only his business philosophy but his faith as well. One was Jim Dubose, a banker.

Bankers, by nature, are skeptics. They have to be. They hold a public trust and must protect money other people place within their vaults. Cecil was keen to this trust placed in bankers and made great efforts to live up to his promises to them. This impressed Jim Dubose, who worked for the Decatur Savings and Loan Bank in Atlanta. Jim loaned Cecil money during his beginnings as an apartment builder and developer of Jiffy's and Carrol's Drive-Ins.

Cecil hired Jim away from the banking business. This move enabled Cecil to bring into his company a man with unique banking skills that later helped thrust Days Inns into the national spotlight.

"I left Decatur Federal Bank," Dubose said years later, "because I liked the way Cecil did business. He was respected within the banking community. Even when he didn't have all the cash necessary to make a payment on a note the day it was due, he met with us, showed us what he planned to do and how he intended to repay his loan. Certainly, we would have preferred a check for the whole amount, but Cecil Day lived up to his pledges.

"Cecil was an honest, hard worker who enjoyed sharing financial gains with his employees rather than hoarding such victories for himself. He was generous in a unique way, allowing others within the rank and file of his companies to grow to their highest potentials.

"One thing that particularly impressed me about Cecil occurred when we traveled together. Not one night did he go to sleep without kneeling beside his motel bed and praying for each of his family members by name. This example helped me grow with a new appreciation of my own family, as I began praying for them. Cecil even prayed before entering an enterprise or applying for a loan. He sought God's direction in every aspect of his personal and professional life."

In 1971, Jim Dubose headed the Day Mortgage Company, which was another part of an inner-company enterprise Cecil created. Rather than pay other banks discount points, Day Mortgage Company secured loans for Cecil and franchisees more expediently—while saving them money and time, thus promoting the Days Inns expansion program.

During Dubose's tenure as president and director of Day Mortgage, his division of Cecil's sprawling enterprise secured over $330 million in construction and permanent financing for Cecil, Days Inns and franchisees.

"I knew Cecil as a business partner and a prayer partner. He was a man who once came to my bank to borrow money," Dubose confessed later. "He later hired me to *make* money borrowing money *for* him. Best of all, he was my friend."

Roy Burnette

Cecil had to find each employee's "hot button." Some of his workers were driven by money; some merely wanted to be independent; others were motivated totally out of loyalty to Day.

One of the talents Cecil Day developed was an uncanny ability to size up an individual. After a ten-minute conversation, he could pinpoint a person's need and what it would take to motivate him.

Late one afternoon in May 1973, Cecil rushed through the closing doors of a Delta jet departing Dallas for Orlando. He held tightly a set of blueprints and his boarding pass for the last seat available on the aircraft.

The jet began moving as Day buckled himself into his aisle seat.

"Whoa!" he panted to a stranger beside him. "I almost missed this flight."

The man sitting in the middle seat, wearing the uniform

of an Air Force captain, nodded with a "you-should-have-been-here-earlier" smirk on his face and continued reading his newspaper.

"Have you ever been to Viet Nam?" pried Cecil.

"Yep," said the stranger, as he hid behind his paper. "Several times."

Cecil stretched out his hand to him. "I'd like to thank you for what you've done for our country."

Touched by this expression of gratitude from a citizen during an unpopular war, the serviceman accepted Cecil's handshake. "Thanks," he said. "I usually only hear that from my parents and wife."

"My name is Cecil Day."

"Glad to meet you, Cecil. I'm Roy Burnette."

Burnette introduced Phyllis, his lovely bride of six months. For the remainder of the flight, Day and Burnette compared experiences. Cecil told Roy how he served in the Marine Corps. They exchanged war stories.

Where did you attend school?" asked Cecil.

"I graduated from Georgia Tech in '67."

"Are you serious?" Cecil chuckled. "I graduated from there in '58."

They exchanged more war stories—this time about the rigors of Tech.

"By the way," asked Roy, "what do you do?"

"Oh, I'm involved with a little motel chain." Cecil explained that he was en route to Orlando for a meeting to explain a ten-year plan. "Here's the type of motel we're building," he said, as he reached beneath his seat for a set of blueprints.

"I never heard of these Days Inns before," Roy said, "but I wish your company luck with them."

"Roy, there are some people on this plane who will be at that meeting. Come on. I'd like to introduce you to them."

Reluctantly, Roy stood and followed Cecil down the aisle,

as he introduced the highly decorated airman to employees. After they returned to their seats, Cecil invited Roy to join him for breakfast in Orlando the next morning.

"There's one problem with that," Roy warned. "I've got to be on my base by noon. I'm processing out of the military tomorrow, and I can't be late."

"How about meeting me at the Sheraton on the Beeline Expressway at 7:30 in the morning, then?"

"Uh . . . that'll be fine," said Roy, still uncertain about the aggressive style of the man he met less than an hour ago.

But things weren't so fine for Roy Burnette that evening. He spent most of the night suffering from food poisoning he had gotten from dinner.

"So much for your meeting with that guy in the morning," said Phyllis.

"Yeah," agreed Roy. "It sure looks that way."

By morning, Roy was feeling good enough to show up at the Sheraton at 7:30 sharp. "Something," Roy said, "kept telling me to go anyway." He drove to the Sheraton as invited. When he entered the cafeteria, his face showed the effects of the previous night's illness. What Roy saw didn't make him feel any better. Not one customer was in the cafeteria.

"So, this is what I get for listening to strangers on airplanes," Roy muttered to himself. "I'd rather be back in bed. I'll give this guy one more minute. . . . "

A telephone rang; the cashier behind the counter answered it. "Are you Captain Burnette?" she asked.

"Ah . . . yes."

"There's a Mr. Day on the phone. He says he'll be a little late. He wants you to please wait just a little while longer."

"Tell him I'll be here," said Roy, who was too exhausted to argue.

Five minutes later, Cecil and an entourage of 25 men

walked into the Sheraton. He shook Roy's hand and apologized for his lateness. "After breakfast," he said, "I'd like you to join our meeting."

Roy didn't eat much breakfast, but he did go to the meeting. He was impressed with what he heard.

Later that day he traded his military uniform for a three-piece business suit. His first stop was to the Day Realty of Orlando offices where he was hired as a construction superintendent.

Roy Burnette remained with Days Inns even after the Day family sold it in 1984. He later left his position as chief operations officer for the company and branched out on his own.

Later, Burnette confessed, "I'll always be grateful to Cecil Day and the opportunity he gave me. I've tried emulating his conduct in my business—and it works. My publishing, leasing and corporate finance companies are doing well. I owe so much to Cecil's faith in me."

The "Encourager"

Not everyone who succeeded under Cecil Day's guidance came to him with flying credentials. Many were humble people with dreams who just wanted to do the best they could with what the Good Lord gave them. One such person was Betty Jean Crawford, a former waitress at a Tasty World restaurant in Atlanta. To this day, she likes to tell her own story.

"One night back in '73, we were just cleaning up the Tasty World. I was the last waitress working that evening. We closed the restaurant at ten o'clock as directed by our manager. About 15 minutes later, a man wearing white shorts, scuffed tennis shoes and a blue knit shirt knocked on the door.

"I unlocked it. 'Sorry,' I said, 'but we're closed.'

"The stranger looked at me and chuckled. 'Who makes the rules around here?' he asked with a twinkle in his eye.

" 'I'm sorry, sir,' I repeated, 'but we're closed for the evening. Will you visit us tomorrow? We open at six.'

"The man paused before speaking. 'What's your name?' he asked with a gentle tone in his voice.

"I almost felt sorry for the man. He acted as though he was real hungry. 'Betty Jean Crawford,' I told him. 'My friends call me "BJ." '

"The stranger smiled. He had a real friendly type of smile— the down-to-earth kind. He extended his hand in a business-like manner. 'I'm Cecil Day,' he said. 'It's good to meet you, Betty Jean Crawford.'

" 'Oh, Lordy!' I thought to myself. 'I'm gonna get fired tomorrow for telling the owner he can't come into his own place.'

"Mr. Day walked on in and looked around. He commented on how clean everything was. Just like that, he left and said, 'Hope to see you again, B.J.'

"I continued working as a Tasty World waitress until eight months later when Mr. Day dropped by for lunch. This time he wore a suit and tie. It wasn't real busy, and he asked me how things were going. I told him things were rather slow that particular day. Then he caught me off-guard with a question right out of the blue. 'B.J., have you ever thought of going into the restaurant business for yourself? I bet you'd be good at it.'

"I was shocked! All my life that had been my dream. I wondered how he knew.

"Mr. Day asked me to sit down. For about an hour I told him what I hoped to do. He listened to every word I said as he ate his hamburger. He finished lunch, com-plimented the cook, paid for his meal and went back to his main offices on Buford Highway.

"One week later, he came back in. He made a business proposal to me to work as a waitress in one of his Jiffy restaurants on the other side of Atlanta. I took the offer.

One year later, he leased me the building. It was mine to run and operate. Before long, I was making more money out of that little 32-seat restaurant than I ever dreamed possible.

"Mr. Day would stop by every now and then. He encouraged me and told me how proud he was for me. That made me work even harder.

"When Mr. Day died, my heart almost broke in two. I went to his funeral. I realized at that moment how important it is to have encouragers. That's how I remember him—'Encourager.' "

Others Followed

Day continued using his ability to cast people for specific jobs, thus expanding his businesses the way the matchmaker in *Fiddler on the Roof* arranged marriages. Employees who knew him well enough often approached Cecil with their own ideas of what the company needed and offered themselves as solutions. If Cecil agreed, he set up a company for them to operate. Most often, however, he envisioned the idea for a new company and placed the person he thought most fit to run it profitably.

He sent Richard Kessler to set up Day Realty of Orlando. Kessler's mission was to saturate the area around the new home of Walt Disney World with Days Inns.

Cliff Gilbreath was sent to Savannah to build apartments and motels. Nick Powell went to Albany to construct apartments, operate motels and invest in real estate. In Atlanta, Day left the operations of Day Realty to his brother, Lon.

Bill Hitson, James Frame and Tom Wright were sent to Dallas to "win the West." These men were to build a west-to-east link of motels along major east-west interstates leading to and from Walt Disney World.

Cecil sent Dick Boyer to North Carolina to "kick up some dust," build and operate motels and apartments for

Day Realty of Charlotte. Kingston Howard was hired away from Howard Johnson's to open Day Realty of New England.

The Golden Noose

As each man left Atlanta to head a new venture, he carried with him what Cecil Day called his "golden noose." When Cecil saw a unique individual he wanted to keep, he slipped an invisible "noose" around his neck to keep him committed to a program. The noose was in the form of a golden opportunity for the man who was given up to 30 percent ownership of the new company for as long as the enterprise yielded acceptable financial results.

Day placed a lot of responsibility for controlling the expanding empire into the steady hands of Bob Williams—once that Carrol's hamburger cook from Augusta. From the home offices in Atlanta, Williams grabbed the opportunity and helped Cecil fortify the Day companies' overall operations.

Were there risks in trusting so many people with his money? "Yes," admitted Day. "The sad news is that it failed ten percent of the time; the great news is that it worked 90 percent of the time."

Bob Dollar's $12.95 Franchising School

Rev. Bob Dollar, a former missionary to Venezuela, joined the Day Team early in 1969, along with his wife, Jo. Both attended Mercer University in Macon while Cecil and Deen were students there.

When the Days Inns totaled 14 properties, Bob Dollar stopped Cecil in the hallway with a quick idea. "Cecil, we ought to consider franchising Days Inns. I'm getting a lot of inquiries about that from all across the country."

Cecil hesitated and thought back to his dismal experience as a franchisee of Carrol's and Jiffy's restaurants.

Franchising carried with it both a plus and a minus side.

On one hand, total ownership of the properties meant total control with all the profits going to the company. Franchising is a very risky business. Lawsuits fill courtrooms from disenchanted franchisees claiming that a franchisor painted a "pie-in-the-sky" picture of wealth. On the other hand, when a Days Inns franchisee brings a single motel out of the ground, the company receives about $50,000 a year in royalties. Over a 20-year term, that adds up to a lot of money. It's like having a one million dollar debt-free asset. Additionally, it would expand interstate exposure more quickly than if the company attempted it by itself.

"Bob," said Cecil, "let's hold off another year before we do any franchising."

"Okay, Cecil. But when we get to that point, I'd like to throw my hat in the ring as one to head it up."

Just one week later, Cecil saw Dollar in the Day Realty Building coffee shop. He walked over to him and slapped him on the back.

"Congratulations, Bob," Cecil chimed. "You're now vice president and director of franchising."

Cecil sat in a chair next to the stunned Dollar.

"Bob, let's make it our goal to process at least thirty franchises a year."

Coffee spewed from Dollar's mouth.

"Thirty!" gasped Bob. "That's pretty aggressive. Are you serious?"

Cecil smiled, said nothing, got up and left for his office.

It was another typical Cecil Day move. He had a missionary fresh out of the steamy jungles of South America heading a brand new franchising department. Cecil's decision had others within his own ranks shaking their heads in disbelief.

But Cecil Day knew what he was doing.

"People who are in God's business are accustomed to placing others first. By serving God, they are actually in the people business. Since the hospitality business is a people business, I think they are uniquely qualified."

Dollar was never taught about franchising in seminary. He went to the nearest bookstore and paid $12.95 (plus tax) for a book about franchising. He absorbed the lessons from the book's chapters and put them into action.

Within three months, the franchising department grew so fast that it had to be divided into three divisions: sales, development and operations.

Even Cecil Day was impressed. He stopped by Bob's office with an offer.

"Bob, I'm going to give you a choice. You've done well putting these franchises together. I have a proposition for you. There are commissions to be made in sales. You can head up all three divisions as you're now doing or go strictly into sales."

Day paused and looked Dollar squarely in the eye.

"So, Bob, what'll it be? Money or power?"

Dollar chuckled. "When you put it that way, Cecil, I'll take sales."

Dollar's remarkable record of sales—150 franchises, without *any* litigation—was, and still is, something unheard of in the franchising industry.

Cecil Day later remarked, "That little $12.95 book on franchising sure paid off for *everyone*."

The Best of Times; the Worst of Times

For three years a trio sang "Happy Days Are Here Again" at the annual Christmas banquets hosted for employees and friends of Days Inns by Cecil. Nationally known personalities such as Paul Harvey and Art Linkletter spoke at the banquets, praising the vision of Cecil Day and congratulating the employees on their superb accomplishments.

The banquets were always well attended, partly because Cecil personally paid the traveling and lodging expenses for each motel's manager and spouse. Joining the managers at these no-alcohol functions were bankers, franchisees, vendors, relatives and others with whom Cecil conducted business.

The singing continued long after the last person left the banquet hall. Day's dreams soared like a kite higher and higher. He added more balls of string each time the end of one appeared.

Suddenly, overnight, the singing stopped. Employees stared at each other in disbelief. The Arab oil embargo hit Day's kite in November 1973 like a sidewinder missile hurled from across the Atlantic. Some employees panicked. A few cried. Others ran for cover.

Cecil Day didn't budge one inch. For a brief moment he grimaced when his kite suddenly nosedived to the ground. He was tempted to let go, but in his heart was the persistent "tug" that kept him stable.

The Marine in Day suddenly snapped to attention. He remembered the voice of his father saying again, "Keep on keepin' on."

The kite was financially too heavy to remain aloft. So Cecil reduced the weight by first cutting his own salary to only $100 a week. He continued to draw that salary for the next 18 months. Next, he reduced the salaries of employees— beginning with upper management. Many upper level employees agreed to work at lower jobs. He moved even one of his sons—Burke—from the main office to a lesser paying job at the reservations center.

Day sensed the threat of panic in the air. He wrote notes of encouragement to his staff and articles in the inner-company newsletter, *Days World*. Cecil stressed that the embargo was temporary and would eventually pass.

He traveled expressways by car, stopping at each exit where he saw a Days Inn sign towering above a motel. He talked to managers over a cup of coffee. Often he invited cooks, waiters and waitresses to join him at the table. He used his special brand of humor to keep the informal sessions light.

His employees out in the field needed his assistance. Many bankers were edgy about the declining occupancy at Days Inns and the lodging industry at large. Some threatened foreclosure on notes that were paid late or not in full.

For the next three years, Cecil visited at least three bankers a day. His greatest personal concern was that he might be unable to pay one banker demanding full payment on a note. If this happened, other bankers would panic and follow suit, and Days Inns signs would topple like dominoes.

More Problems

Many of his team members burned out while assisting Cecil's efforts to keep his kite flying. An even greater burden fell upon his shoulders when most of the five founding members developed problems. One suffered several major heart attacks and could not work. Another was overly burdened with financial problems of his own. Two left for personal reasons.

Cecil Day was left alone.

Day Realty of Dallas was hit especially hard during the embargo. Not only was it a new company whose president had just resigned, but it was deeply in debt owing to an ambitious construction program. The bankers certainly knew everything about Day's financial statement, but very little about his character.

James Frame became president of Day Realty of Dallas. Frame, no stranger to Texas, personally visited bankers to keep them calm about the oil crisis and to tell them about Cecil's unblemished record of paying his debts on time.

The tension was more than anyone should be expected to handle. Frame neared exhaustion. Cecil flew from Atlanta to Dallas to do what he could to help. The two men and a small staff worked feverishly during their first meeting to formulate solutions to the company's problems.

Two days later, when everyone was present, Day made a surprising announcement: "I want Jim Frame to leave for a solid week, and I don't want *any* of you to call him with any problems. Instead, you call *me* in Atlanta."

Cecil insisted that Frame and his wife take a week's vacation in New Orleans.

"I was so mentally, emotionally and physically exhausted," Frame confessed later, "that I could hardly drive my car. My wife had to do most of the driving to New Orleans. However, that trip was an oasis in a desert for both me and my wife."

Mending Broken Friendships

It happens in practically every business sooner or later. Two people who have worked closely together to shape a young company have a disagreement about policy. A discussion turns into a debate; the debate evolves into an argument; the argument becomes a fight; the fight KO's a once-rewarding relationship. The winner stands alone with his arms raised signaling victory, while the defeated packs his bags and limps out the door—usually to work for a competing firm.

That's the script for most businesses.

But Cecil Day was not your typical businessman. Instead of gloating over broken relationships, he tried to mend them.

A prime example involved Dave Kenney, Days Inns' president during the hectic days of the Arab oil embargo.

Dave and Cecil formed a perfect match. When Cecil left Scott Hudgens' employ, he took with him salesman Dick Fowler, builder Tom Fuqua and, to complete Day's new team, a top-notch corporate operations man—Dave Kenney.

Kenney had distinguished credits Cecil lacked. Dave worked for his father, one of Howard Johnson's first franchisees, as a cook, busboy and "go-fer." This real-world experience blended with his academic credentials in hotel/restaurant management from Michigan State University.

In the early '60s, Cecil and Dave created an operating company—Jiffy Drive-Ins, Inc.—in which Cecil owned 60 percent and Dave 40 percent. The agreement between the two friends was simple: Cecil would build and develop the restaurants; Dave was to operate and manage the day-by-day operations.

The two men frequently met at five in the morning during those days. It was the best time to speak without interruptions. Communications between them was tight and closely woven. They enjoyed plenty of success with Jiffy Drive-Ins. It was only natural, then, that Cecil carried this arrangement into his new motel venture.

Day personally secured financing for land along the interstates and for the motel buildings. He then leased them to his new operating company—Days Inns. This arrangement resembled that between a landlord and tenant. Dave, as president of Days Inns, was in charge of getting chattel mortgages—loans that financed a motel's furnishings, fixtures and equipment.

The rapid progress of construction and expansion eventually wore on the nerves of the two long-time friends. Expansion also left few opportunities for the two friends to meet as they once did. When they did meet, dialogues that were once light and rewarding were filled with tension. An age-old clash between developer and operations became more and more obvious.

Cecil argued that operations people are too slow and cautious. Dave contended that developers move too quickly and recklessly.

The problems came to a head when the Arab oil embargo hit the nation. Cecil had completed arrangements for most of his loans. Dave was still working on closing his.

Cecil was already cash-thin. He not only personally guaranteed loans for his developed properties on which his motels sat, but also personally guaranteed Days Inns' *corporate* loans. Cecil depended heavily on banks, especially at this juncture. He hoped that Kenney had secured the chattel loans for motels.

Cecil telephoned Kenney, calling a meeting in Day's office on the fourth floor. They didn't discuss victories of yesteryear. Instead, they spoke about survival—corporately and personally.

Cecil lamented that Dave had not kept pace. "When I bring a motel out of the ground," Cecil seethed through his teeth, "I expect you to have your chattel mortgages closed, the money from the loans in the company's bank account and every motel open and operating at 100 percent."

"But Cecil!" Kenney retorted, throwing up his arms in frustration. "I can't make a move unless *you* have the buildings finished. Banks won't lend Days Inns a dime unless the properties are finished."

That argument didn't fly in Cecil's opinion. He considered a motel complete and ready to be occupied as soon as it had running water, functional toilets, bathtubs and a non-leaking roof. He expected Kenney to have sheets on beds that had yet to be financed before the last construction worker picked up his final paycheck.

"Fix the chattel mortgage problems," Cecil demanded, stomping his foot on the floor. "Close those loans and get that money, or I'll get someone else who will."

In less than two months, Dave resigned in protest. He couldn't live on his reduced salary—a sacrifice all employees were forced to make for corporate survival—coupled with Cecil's demands that Kenney secure loans from a depleted banking community, now more nervous than ever about making loans to motels.

When Dave Kenney abruptly emptied his Days Inns office,

Cecil's face sagged. He feared he had lost a dear friend and business associate of 14 years.

Many people let friendships die after such a clash. But Cecil still treasured them. He resolved deep in his heart that he wasn't going to toss out this friendship as he would yesterday's garbage.

During the ensuing months, Day asked his family at the dinner table to pray individually for Dave. Cecil joined the prayers, earnestly asking that God bless Dave who now was in business for himself.

Rather than scratch Kenney's name off invitation lists as Emily Post might have suggested, Cecil purposely kept Dave's name on them. Kenney attended some of those functions at Cecil's invitation. Cecil acknowledged in future discussions with Dave their differences but spoke of other issues on which they agreed. Gradually, the icy wall between them melted.

One afternoon, shortly after Cecil knew of the cancer that would eventually take his life, he and Dave reminisced over lunch about the good things they accomplished individually and together. Cecil congratulated Dave on his new motel management company's success.

On a crisp, fall day in 1988, Dave Kenney demonstrated just how important this friendship was to him, when he walked to a podium at Georgia State University in Atlanta. He leaned over the microphone. After clearing his throat, he spoke softly about his old friend: "There is hardly a day that I don't think of him. He would bring out the best in me and have me walking on clouds. This man had the ability to get the best out of people."

Then Dave Kenney walked over to a tripod covered by a white linen cloth. He pulled it off, unveiling a bronze portrait of the man after which the new school Kenney created was named: THE CECIL B. DAY SCHOOL OF HOSPITALITY ADMINISTRATION.

Remembering Others Always

As busy as he was, Cecil never forgot the needs of his church and other charitable institutions. Even during the hard times of the oil embargo, he continued giving of his time and talents to these causes. The Haggai Institute was one of these organizations to which Cecil pledged himself.

The Haggai Institute, with headquarters in Atlanta, exists for one purpose—to train national leaders of the Third World on how to evangelize in their homelands.

The oil embargo also left its mark on the work of the Haggai Institute, driving up its cost of operation 40 percent. Dr. John Haggai, its founder and president, called an emergency meeting of the board of directors—of which Cecil Day was a member.

"Our financial situation was critical," recalls Haggai. "It was the only time in twenty years that I called for such an emergency meeting. I gave them only a three-hour notice. To clear time was particularly hard for Cecil, since he was fighting his own incredible battles just to keep his motel empire alive and well. Nonetheless, Cecil was there. And he, along with six other men, came up with a solution to our problem in less than twenty minutes.

"As we were leaving the meeting, Cecil turned to me and said, 'I wish I had seven men I could call on to help me in a crisis.'

"Not until that time did I fully grasp the loneliness at the top, and the singular blessing I had of having access to men of Cecil's caliber.

"Though he was a creative loner in business, he was a team player on boards where he held membership."

By 1976, the negative impact of the oil embargo showed signs of rippling away. Some of his associates described Cecil Day as "Motel Moses," because he led his company through the wilderness of doubt and anxiety during three years of crisis. Even bankers, who once wondered if he'd ever make it, had a greater respect for him.

A wise man once said: "We grow only through exposure and conflict." The struggle to survive during the Arab oil embargo did a lot to strengthen not only Cecil but his companies as well. As a result, by 1977, the Day empire had grown beyond all expectation through faith, prayer, loyalty and, of course, teamwork.

10

Reach Beyond a Code of Ethics

Cecil Day was a great-hearted business leader whose exceptional humanitarian concern set the highest standards of corporate responsibility.

—Coretta Scott King

Cecil Day was an "innkeeper on a mission." During the dark times, he was at his creative best. Here, Cecil holds one of the 4,000,000 Bibles given to his motel guests free of charge.

It takes people helping each other during austere periods. During such times we have to be willing to give each other mercy, rather than justice.

—Cecil B. Day

Fewer things were more frightening to Cecil Day than seeing a framed "Code of Ethics" hanging above the desk of someone with whom he was about to conduct business. Immediately he wondered if this was the kind of person who might declare, "I will never lie to you," while seeing nothing wrong with revealing only *part* of the truth. In short, such a person could live up to the *letter* of the law but, by doing so, bypass the *spirit* of the law.

Cecil Day sensed the difference between the two.

Early in 1976, the Day Companies were still rocking from the '73 Arab oil embargo and the tremors of the subsequent economic recession. During this time, Cecil's family rarely saw him. Most of his time was spent visiting at least three nervous bankers a day.

The economic problems of the industry had a direct impact on the Day family as well. During all of 1976 Cecil drew only $100 a week. He bought only the basic necessities for himself and his family. He could not justify wearing a new pair of shoes if he couldn't live up to his financial obligations.

To him, spending money on luxuries was at the expense of a creditor.

In the spring of '76, Day drove from Atlanta to Florida to see a franchisee who owed him over $200,000 in principal and interest.

Day walked into an office, accompanied by his attorneys, and sat at a large oval table. Across the table sat the franchisee with his attorneys. The room was unusually quiet. Rustling stacks of paper occasionally broke the silence.

One of the franchisee's attorneys spoke first. He wanted Day to accept only a portion of the debt. Day's attorneys returned the volley demanding that the note was legal, binding and past due. They wanted the cash paid according to the contract, immediately.

Cecil Day sat quietly.

As the discussion turned into a heated debate, Cecil read the terms of the promissory note to himself. He thought about his creditors and what he owed them, about his family and what he would like to buy them. He thought especially about the upcoming medical expenses for one of his sons stricken with a rare muscle disease that would land him in a wheelchair.

The shouting got louder. Cecil rose from his chair. The room became silent once again.

"Gentlemen," Day said matter-of-factly, "I feel led by the Lord to do this." He pulled a pen from his shirt pocket, leaned over the table and, looking down at the promissory note, wrote something on it. He then removed the jacket he had placed on the back of his chair, slid his arms through its sleeves, picked up his briefcase and walked out of the room, alone.

One of Day's attorneys reached over and picked up the promissory note. His mouth dropped open. He stretched across the table and handed the note to one of the franchisee's attorneys, who scratched his head, shrugged his shoulders and handed it to the franchisee. The franchisee read what Cecil had written. He couldn't believe what he saw. Written across the promissory note in bold letters was the word: "V O I D !"

Cecil later defended his action: "It takes people helping each other during austere periods. During such times we have to be willing to give each other *mercy* rather than *justice*.

"If God gave us all *justice*, we wouldn't deserve very much. Fortunately He deals with us out of *mercy* and *love*. We have to deal with other people the same way."

The "Slice of Bread" Approach

Earlier, Cecil had learned what mercy was about during the Arab oil embargo. Cecil had flown to Texas to see James Frame, president of Day Realty of Dallas. Frame had set up meetings with bankers. Together they met with a few bankers for breakfast, others for lunch, and more for dinner.

Some bankers were willing to work with Cecil; others were not.

Early the next morning Cecil and Jim Frame met with a banker to whom Day owed $75,000 on a $125,000 note. It was time for another quarterly payment. Unfortunately, Day did not have the necessary cash.

Day explained his financial situation to the bank's president. The president leaned back in his brown leather chair, half listening and twiddling his thumbs. "Well," shouted the bank's president, "I'll just have to call the whole note!" Before waiting for any response from Day or Frame, the president stormed out the door to the office of the bank chairman.

Minutes later, the chairman came into the president's office and, like a Marine drill instructor, barked, "You have a financial statement that shows your net worth in the millions of dollars, Mr. Day. And you're telling us you can't pay the $75,000 you owe?"

"That's exactly what I'm telling you," replied Cecil. "I simply don't have the cash to pay you. I owe you the money, I admit that, and I *will* pay you. But . . . it's like a loaf of bread."

"What?" demanded the chairman.

"I can't eat a whole loaf of bread at one time," Day continued, "but I can eat it one slice at a time. If you will just work with me on a 'slice-by-slice' basis, I'm sure I can repay. . . ."

"Not a chance!" interrupted the chairman. He turned to the bank president standing behind him. "There's no reason to discuss this any further. Day owes us money. Call the note. Call our lawyer and file suit!"

Day and Frame slumped in their chairs.

The bank president looked at the chairman. "Let's go into the other room and talk about this. Let's see if we can work something out."

Cecil and Jim could hear the chairman and the president shouting at each other in the next room. "There's nothing more *we* can do," said Cecil, and he dropped to his knees in prayer. Jim Frame joined him. When the shouting next door stopped, the two returned to their seats and waited. The bank president came back into the office.

"The chairman has agreed to eat the note—one slice at a time," he said.

Cecil repaid the entire note three months before it was due.

Cecil later admitted, "Frankly, if people hadn't had confidence and worked patiently with us, I don't think we would have survived the embargo. Their goodness and forbearance kept us going. I'll always be grateful for those who helped us."

Cecil Day was more than a lender and a borrower. He also knew how to make more money by spending money in a fair and equitable way.

The Whole Truth

The Arab oil embargo nearly brought the real estate market to its knees. Brokers were frantic. Homes weren't selling; commercial values stagnated; double-digit inflation headlined the news.

This was the setting when Cecil attended a board of realtors meeting called to discuss ways to survive the real estate crisis. A woman who taught real estate classes to prospective State licensees spoke forcefully from a podium about how to survive the present real estate crunch.

"Do whatever you must do," she spouted into a microphone. "The important thing is to get potential buyers into our homes. Sell them on all the good points of the house and minimize the negative aspects. That is your best bet in landing a sales contract."

A question-answer period followed her thunderous, "sell-'em-what-you-can" speech.

"What about latent defects?" asked a newcomer to the trade. "Aren't we supposed to tell a buyer everything about a house, even its hidden flaws?"

"Accentuate the positives," answered the speaker, winking at the aspiring real estate salesperson. "After all, how can you really determine what is a flaw?"

Cecil stood to make a point. "I think that approach is not only wrong but short-sighted as well," he said.

The speaker laughed nervously.

"Sooner or later, this embargo crisis will run its course," he continued, "and we'll be back to normal. Each of us will still have our names. They should be honorable names, based on dealing honestly with the public."

"Mr. Day," the speaker said slowly and deliberately, "you are going to go out of business with that attitude."

"I don't think so," Day responded matter-of-factly. "The business community quickly weeds out those companies that are not honest. They'll remember who did what. I worked hard to earn an honest name. I refuse to compromise it for the sake of a sale."

Members of the audience applauded.

The speaker looked at them in disbelief. Before abruptly turning to leave the stage, she shouted, "I need a Valium!"

A Real Deal

Late one afternoon, a salesman bounced into Day's office with what he called a fantastic offer. He spread out some plot plans on Cecil's desk.

"What you have here, Cecil, is the deal of the century right before your eyes," declared the salesman, pointing to a piece of property on the plans.

Day carefully studied the plans, paying particular attention to the cost of the property he hoped to buy. Then he looked at the properties surrounding the one he wanted and noticed that they were listed at twice the price.

"Is there anything wrong or unusual about the piece I want?" Day asked.

"Nope, not a thing," answered the salesman. "The owners live in some old shack and, between you and me, they're about as smart as a sack of hammers."

"Are they sane?" Day asked.

"As far as I can tell," said the salesman.

Cecil leaned back in his chair and looked toward the ceiling. "Something isn't right about this," he concluded.

"You better hurry up and buy it before someone else does," the salesman said. "At this price, it'll sell fast."

Later that week, Cecil drove to the property. Cecil saw no reason why the property he wanted was selling so much cheaper than the adjacent parcels. He thought it would be best were he to visit the owners.

The owners were much like the salesman described. It was obvious to Day that they had little education. He learned that the land on which they lived had been in their family through four generations.

Standing on the front porch of the rotting, clapboard house, Cecil spoke with the owners.

"Why are you selling your land so cheap?" Cecil asked earnestly.

"Ain't much good fer nothin' no mo'," replied the owner. "Ust to be that you could bring in t'maters by hundreds o' bushels. Now we're lucky ta git a dozen or so."

Cecil smiled, shook the farmer's hand and left for Atlanta.

When the salesman entered Cecil's office the next day, he could tell Cecil was disturbed.

"What's the matter, Cecil? Didn't I tell you the truth about that place?" He quickly placed a contract before Cecil to sign. "It's a steal!"

Day looked at the contract, then at the salesman. He picked up the contract and, in front of the salesman, tore it up and threw it into the wastebasket.

"Wha . . . What did you do that for?" asked the wide-eyed salesman.

Day's face hardened like plaster. "That property is worth just as much as the land surrounding it. It's that simple."

"But, Cecil, this is a great deal!" pleaded the frustrated salesman, who now wished that he had stayed in bed that morning.

"This is no deal," blurted Cecil. "Remember, a deal is a deal only when it's a good deal for both parties. Otherwise, as you say, it's a 'steal.' Thieves steal. That's not the kind of businessman I am."

A new contract was drawn up and Day bought the property for twice the asking price. He still got his money's worth. That property is now the site of a Days Inn.

Cecil Day needed no framed code of ethics.

11

Make the System Work for You

> *Cecil Day showed that you do not need to compromise your values in order to succeed.*
>
> —Rev. Billy Graham

Days Inns corporate headquarters houses all administrative and executive offices.

There was nothing new or fancy about what Cecil Day accomplished. He just did it.

> —Furman H. Agee III,
> Executive Vice President,
> Cecil B. Day Investment Company

Within a span of only eight years, Cecil Day constructed a chain of 301 motels, with over 42,000 rooms. Before his death from bone cancer at age 44, he left a legacy that still serves conscientious business people throughout the world.

That legacy may not guarantee that we will all become instant millionaires, but it can help make us better candidates for success in business and life.

Dare to Do the Impossible

In a collegiate basketball gymnasium, Cecil Day could have turned his back and walked away from the young co-ed a friend described as "unreachable." Yet he bucked the odds. He wasn't afraid to ask for big favors. He realized the worst that could happen was to be told, "No." His willingness to dare gained him his most valuable treasure—his wife, Deen.

When he came face-to-face with giants who stood between him and his goals, he rarely allowed them to control him; instead, he made them work *for* him. He channeled the same adrenaline that would have made others run away into a productive, well supervised "internal steam machine" that propelled him forward.

Refuse to Quit

Cecil could have thrown his hands up in surrender when he was booted out of college. Instead, he looked for a way to reach his dream of attending Georgia Tech. He joined the Marine Corps, which pressure-cooked him not only into a disciplined student but into a tenacious businessman as well.

When he flunked his first real estate endeavor, he took a few steps back, lowered his head, then rammed harder into his next attempt, until he won. It was a philosophy he learned from his father and shared with his children and employees— "Keep on keepin' on."

Create Your Own Opportunities

While others held committee meetings in an attempt to look for ways to build a better mousetrap, Cecil simply rolled up his sleeves and worked. Most of those who knew him were constantly amazed that one man could do so much in such a short time. However, as Furman Agee said, "There was nothing new or fancy about what Cecil Day accomplished. He just did it."

He never believed that a closed door signaled finality to an endeavor. He learned to listen to the noise of a hard-slammed door and see which window was left open. For him, this meant taking action to solve problems rather than complain about them.

During the Arab oil embargo, for example, he created the "September Days Club." The membership of this loyal organization accounted for 50 percent of his motel occupancy during the especially hard times of the embargo. It all started with his idea of offering a "wooden nickel" to senior citizens.

Identify What's Really Important

Identifying what was really important was a crucial element of Cecil Day's success. And he had a simple way of remembering what was important—a legal-sized notepad. Day operated his offices, kept bank note due dates and appointments written down in a notepad that seldom left his side. He knew that not being organized would result in his life floating like a stringless kite. That notepad helped him make each step count.

Establish a Sense of Values

A proper sense of values formed the foundation for Cecil Day's success. He learned these values in church. Every business guideline for him was already set in the Bible. He believed that biblical principles formed the foundation of any business that longed for success. From the Bible he learned that lying, stealing and selfishness not only were morally wrong but also spelled failure in any business or personal relationship.

One of the unique qualities of Cecil Day was his willingness to reach beyond the technicalities printed in a framed "code of ethics" hanging on the wall above a desk. He treated his business office as he would his personal home. Just as he never cheated his family, so he dealt squarely with his business associates. His favorite motto, "A deal is not a deal unless it's a good deal for both parties," was more than a mere expression. He lived it.

Pay Your Debts

Times were not always easy for Cecil Day. But he was able to endure hard times partly because others knew he would pay them what he owed. By maintaining good relationships with vendors, bankers and others to whom he owed

money, Day kept his kite aloft—even in the face of the Arab
oil embargo.

He truly believed that people, by nature, were good and
deserved trust. When the time came for Cecil to ask the
same of others, they trusted him in return. During lean times,
when he couldn't meet all his payments that were due, he
reworked plans with his debtors and never hid behind the
skirts of Chapter 11 bankruptcy protection although many
financial advisors strongly suggested he do just that.

Keep Your Ego in Check

Cecil Day had a champion's pride. He was keenly aware
of the fact that he could win, while others were satisfied
to gain a tie. He had a healthy confidence in his own abilities,
but at the same time, he knew he could not do it all alone.
He valued a productive team. He therefore offered his
employees a working environment that nurtured loyalty and
challenged them to do their best.

Those who took the opportunity to excel were generously
rewarded. In fact, Cecil's face glowed most when he cel-
ebrated an employee's success.

*   *   *   *   *

If Cecil Day were to wish a legacy to succeed him, it
would not be in marble monuments or granite statues. It
would be a statement suggesting that people search for the
truth in all things; seek out God for the revelation of that
truth; be a good spouse and parent; and, if you wish to
excel in any endeavor, put your ego on the shelf, bow first
to God, then serve others with the talents the Good Lord
gave you. Finally, don't be shocked when it all works for
you and exceeds your wildest dreams.

The simple steps of Cecil Day worked for him. He'd be
the first to say they can work for *you*.

EPILOGUE

> Cecil Day proved that dreams, when combined with positive action, are reachable. His honorable business conduct, his charitable grace and devoted love for God and man made Days Inns a successful reality.
>
> —Kemmons Wilson

Cecil Burke Day, Sr.,
December 10, 1934–December 15, 1978
"A Christian Steward saved by the grace of God."

Dateline: February 9, 1990

I am sitting with my family in the front row of a huge ballroom in Atlanta filled with over 1,000 Days Inns franchisees. Four 12-foot-high gold letters stand on the stage, spelling out D-A-Y-S. A black backdrop makes the letters look even bolder.

Michael A. Leven, Days Inns' president, is speaking gently but with conviction about my father as a role model. "By remaining in the people-caring business as did its founder," he says, "Days Inns will remain ahead of the pack."

"Where has the time gone?" I ask myself. "This is Days Inns' 20th birthday."

Mr. Leven has just finished speaking. We are shown six of the upcoming year's televison ads. Each promotion is met with roaring applause.

Following a coffee break, Mike Leven steps back onto the stage. The room falls quiet in anticipation.

"Ladies and Gentlemen," Mr. Leven says, sweeping his hand to stage left, "President Ronald Reagan."

A spotlight shines on the former president as he walks across the stage and shakes the hand of Michael Leven.

The president steps up to the podium, acknowledges the standing ovation, then speaks heart-to-heart to the audience about the value of entrepreneurs. He begins, "When Cecil Day built his first Days Inns . . ."

I can't help but think about what has happened in the past 20 years. The first motel on Tybee Island . . . the rapid growth . . . the frustrations of the oil embargo . . . the death of my father . . . and the expansion since. It all passed by quickly. Very quickly.

Only seven years ago, our mother, Deen Day Smith, called us children into the den of the home where we were reared and shared a secret. "Just before your father died," she said, "he told me to hold onto the motel chain for five years, then sell it. How do you feel about that?"

Mom was able to maintain the people-centered philosophy on which the company was built. And that wasn't by accident. She and Dad openly discussed the future when it became obvious that his days were numbered. The "glory" position was given to a newly-appointed CEO of Days Inns. Mom held the "power" position as CEO of the Cecil B. Day Companies—the holding company that owned 80 percent of Days Inns. Dad suggested that she sell both companies in five years.

It was the perfect game plan.

That's genius at work. Dad was planning for the future even when he knew he was dying.

In 1984, Mom sold the company for $639 million (including liabilities) to the Reliance Capital Group. They ushered in a sharp-minded, warm-hearted president, Michael Leven.

Under Leven's direction, Days Inns reached my father's dream of 1,000 motels by 1990.

While Days Inns continues to grow, so does the caring philosophy begun by its founder. National television newscasters report on Days Inns' hiring of the homeless, senior citizens and the physically impaired.

A guest on *The Oprah Winfrey Show* singled out Days Inns as the only company in America that does anything about the homeless. That observation is well founded. As a matter-of-fact, Michael Leven created the Cecil B. Day Humanitarian Award—given each year to two franchisees who have done most for these people in their respective communities.

In 1989, the company received over two dozen awards for meritorious accomplishments in humanitarian fields.

When 33-year-old John Snodgrass became Days Inns president in May 1990, less than a year after the company was sold to Tollman-Hundley, he pledged to carry forward the basic philosophies of Mr. Leven and the company's founder. Mr. Snodgrass plans to expand Days Inns in the United States, Canada and throughout the world. In 1994, a ribbon will be cut for the 2,000th Days Inn.

Cecil Day was not able to see his goal of 1,000 motels because of his early death from cancer, but his dream remains aloft through those who now feel the same tug of the kite string.

As a result, Cecil Day's kite continues to fly . . . higher . . . and farther . . . than ever before.

Way to go, Dad.

INDEX